I'm getting a bad reception:

Confessions of an (occasional) wedding DJ

By Matt Engel

I'm getting a bad reception: Confessions of an (occasional) wedding DJ

ISBN: 978-1-4357-1496-0

Table of Contents

Other works by Matt Engel:

<u>Books</u>

Cheaper than therapy: A journey to Waterloo

<u>Periodicals</u>

The Laugh Letter – A monthly comedy newsletter
     Subscription: 12 issues for $15.00

<u>Plays</u>

Ah, suite mystery! – A comedy in three acts

Goodnight Irene – aka Leave it to Beaver Island –
A comedy

Murder a the Head of the Class – A comedy

The Rainbow Man – A comedy.

For more information on *The Music and M. E. Disc*
Jockey Service – please write to:

> **Matt Engel**
> **P. O. Box 1013**
> **Gaylord, Mi 49734**
>
> **www.mattengel.org**

Introduction

'So you wanna be a rock and roll star'

Those are great lyrics from a vintage 1960's tune by the Byrds, but if you actually DO want to be said rock and roll star, then you are reading the wrong book. This book is about the adventures of a mobile disc jockey from Northern Lower Michigan.

A mobile disc jockey is anyone who packs up his or her kit and kaboodle and sets off to play music for any number of occasions. If by chance you have lost either your kit or your kaboodle, I believe they have them in stock at Walmart.

The mobile disc jockey has been around since the caveman days, when Ogg paid Nogg to stand in the corner of the cave and hit a rock with a stick while the other cave people danced. DJ's did not get paid much in those days and if they performed poorly they were probably clubbed to death or eaten by a passing dinosaur. I have played many parties feeling like I have either been clubbed or eaten up myself so I know the feeling. A few of those parties are depicted in this book.

* * * * *

I'm getting a bad reception

My name is Matt Engel and occasionally I play music for weddings and other parties in Northern Lower Michigan under the name of *The Music and M. E. Disc Jockey Service.* I say 'occasionally' because I have a full time, 40 hour a week job.

I remember being a fan of all genres of music since I was young. Every so often I pack up bag and baggage and go into a hall and share my music with a group of strangers, and some are stranger than others as you will soon discover.

What you are about to read is a humorous potpourri of stories from ten years of spinning the platters. It is not in any way intended to be a 'How to' book for the novice who wishes to be a DJ. There are many wonderful books available for that purpose but this is not one of them.

* * * * *

This book is divided into two sections. The first section is called *I'm getting my act together and taking it on the road.* It tells my story of becoming a member of a local singles group, buying sound equipment and music, then getting bookings and playing my first dance. The second section of this book is called *Anatomy of a wedding.* The chapters are laid out as an outline of a typical wedding day. There are stories of playing music at the ceremony, continuing through the various elements that make up the reception, and on to the end of the night. It is quite an adventure and I am glad you came along for the ride.

* * * * *

The events in this book are true. The names and certain situations have been changed to save me from having to appear on *Judge Judy* or *The People's Court* or any time soon.

Thank you for you time.

Enjoy

Matt Engel

No party animals were harmed in the making of this publication.

I'm getting my act together and taking it on the road

'And I knew if I had my chance

That I could make those people dance

And maybe they'd be happy for awhile'

-----Don Mclean 'American Pie'

1

In the beginning,
I'm single let's mingle

My first spark of interest in being a mobile disc jockey came to me when I was involved in a local singles group in Gaylord, Michigan; which I have called home since moving here in 1986. My sister who was newly divorced at the time, told me about the group, and that they were a lot of fun and suggested I join.

The group went out quite a lot and took many road trips. The big events were the semi annual, bi weekly or whenever there was a blue moon, singles dances. Those were held in a large meeting room at the Otsego County Fire Hall in Gaylord. The room was a rather sterile affair and seemed quite uninviting at first glance. People voted in that room and I wondered how they would possibly dance there.

One night, curiosity got the best of me and I tagged along with my sister and her friend Melvin. He was 50 something and divorced. My sister met him in a divorce support group called B. E., for *Beginning Experience*. I often joked that B. E. stood for *Breaking and Entering*.

Admission to the dances was five dollars. You paid at a table by the front door. Somebody had a roll of tickets so dancers could take a chance on a 50/50 drawing. Off to one side was a table full of light snacks and finger foods, with soft drinks and coffee at another. Other than that it was BYOB.

The entertainment varied, first there was a two-piece combo. They were very good and played and sang every song you would ever want to dance too, from standards to rock to country and everything in between. They were a welcome addition to the dances. We had three DJ's come in and play at various times over the weeks and months. Two of them were entertaining and great fun, the other one just sat there like a lump of coal in an uncomfortable suit.

Our regular DJ was named Steve. He was a nice young man in his twenties who looked no more than 14. He had a nice collection of DJ equipment. There was a box about four feet high that unfolded and had a shelf built in where he had two turntables and a sound mixer. He had two large speakers on stands and some stage lights that flashed in time to the music, and a mirrored ball with a light shining on it that sent the glimmer of white dots shooting into every corner of the room.

Eventually I joined the group and discovered that they were indeed a lot of fun. We had a few house parties and went everywhere together. We played cards, went on picnics, went canoeing, camping and shopping. And there were the dances, which were always a blast. I became the editor and publisher of the newsletter, which I wrote quite tongue in cheek and got a lot of nice comments about it.

Periodically we'd carpool over to Traverse City, about 70 miles to the west, for a night on the town at Dill's Old Town Saloon. Dill's had a ragtime house band that put on a rousing show called *The Golden Garter Revue*. They also had a bawdy karaoke hostess nicknamed *Laura The Karaoke Princess*. She was a laugh riot and great fun. She reminded me of a latter day Rusty Warren or Sophie Tucker. A good time was guaranteed for all when you spent a few hours with the Princess. My sister and I would get up on stage and sing *I got you babe* and it brought the house down. It also brought ME down. The music would start and the lyrics would dance across the screen and I would drop to my knees as Sonny Bono while my sister stood next to me as Cher.

I'm getting a bad reception

The singles group began in February 1995. From the beginning, then slowly at first, and oh so surely, the group was headed the way of the dinosaur. And that dinosaur was named Louise, the woman who created the group with her cronies and ran it like a tight fisted South American military leader. Louise was in her mid 50's and had this permanent, puzzled expression on her face that a dog has when you close your hands and it tries to figure out which hand the ball is in.

Louise ran the group but she was not a leader. The singles club had a board, or committee or some such but she did not use them to their fullest potential. Louise did things her way and wouldn't let the board do anything. She was not open to new ideas and fought them tooth and nail. So naturally things went downhill. The group that once went out all the time and spent most of their nights and weekends together did nothing but have dances. The dinosaur was on its way to die in the tar pits.

Louise and her cronies ran the dances (for singles 21 and older, and in some cases WAY over) as if they were running the junior high school homecoming dance. She was ridiculously strict with a group of adults. It wasn't much fun working with her since she was not open to suggestions. At one tempestuous meeting her entire board, my sister and I included, quit on her and formed our own group. We had the greatest of intentions but nothing came of it. I was the only one who went back to Louise and her sinking ship of fools but it was not the same. The dances became more infrequent as people were pairing up and getting married as if that was a requirement for membership. There were more pair ups than on Noah's ark. Each dance was like a wheezy old train making that last stop at Desperation Station.

There was backbiting and in fighting, there was disorganization in the organization. And there, swimming in the eye of the tempest of tension and dissention, was Clara.

Clara was a widow. Clara was a short little gal somewhere between 65 and 300 years old. Clara was the spitting image of Clara Peller, the 'Where's the beef' lady from the Burger King commercials in the 1980's.

Clara was a dancing fool. She loved to dance more than anyone I have ever met. It didn't matter with who, guys, gals, a chair, if it had a beat, Clara was out on the floor. I think you could have tapped a pencil on a card table in rhythm, and she would have been out there dancing to it.

Clara had a good beat and you could dance to her.

So I gave her an 85.

Clara was supposedly second in command of the singles group. Louise kept Clara at arms length regarding income and expenses and finances and every major decision regarding the group. Picture George Bush telling Dick Cheney about the nuclear 'button' but not telling him where it was. One thing in Clara's favor was that she worked her tail off at the dances. She helped set up the tables and put chairs away and so on. I think if she could have re shingled the roof and waxed the floor she would have done that too.

There was a definite power struggle between Louise and Clara. Clara wanted to be in charge of the singles group the way Eva Peron wanted to be in charge of Argentina. Clara lusted for power and Louise was either too dense or too selfish to give it to her. As the group limped along to its inevitable extinction, there were too many kooks, and too many cooks.

As the twilight of the singles group was on the horizon, the dances moved from the local fire hall, to the main showroom of a local restaurant and lounge called Palmer's Place.

Palmer's Place sprang up one sunny day at the former Chalet Restaurant in Gaylord. Palmer's was attached to what was once called the Chalet Motel, which became the Comfort Inn, which became the Super 8. Like every other business in Gaylord, the facade of Palmer's Place and the neighboring hotel buildings were designed to simulate the Alpine look of a Swiss Village.

The Chalet restaurant, which at one time had an incredible nachos platter (take that Taco Bell), closed in the late 1980's. The Palmer's bought the place and pumped new life, and a lot of money into it. In its heyday, Palmer's was the hotspot in Gaylord.

In the front of the building, with a sun terrace and a gorgeous view of the Marathon Gas Station across the street, was the main dining room. The food was outstanding. For breakfast they served the best homemade bread this side of your Grandma's kitchen.

Tucked away from the dining room was the cozy little *Cheers* type bar. The pub was small and everybody indeed knew your name. And they could sit close enough to count every hair on your head. But the pub was a comfortable place. There was a pinball machine, jukebox, dartboard and a pool table. Off in a corner was a small stage where thousands of good rock, pop and country tunes were massacred by well meaning karaoke singers.

In the back were meeting rooms with a buffet. In the very back was the showroom. If Palmer's was a Las Vegas property, that would have been the 'main room'. The stage in the corner played host to everything from stand up comics, heavy metal bands, country music, line dance classes, stage plays including Neil Simon's *The Sunshine Boys,* and everything in between.

> 'I know a place
> Where the music is fine and the lights are always low
> I know a place where we can go'
> ------Petula Clark

And go we did, nearly every weekend for a while, to see and be seen. But alas, it has been said that all good things must come to an end. Slowly and surely, yet again, it did at Palmer's Place. The Palmer's divorced, yet still operated their place. Soon however the bands stopped playing, the stand up comics stood up somewhere else and even the karaoke stage wasn't fun anymore.

Even our great, fun, singles club did nothing more than the aforementioned dances. People stopped coming. With smaller crowds, the club couldn't afford the higher priced DJ's it once had. The quality of the entertainment slowly diminished as well.

In the fall of 1996 the singles club held its very last dance in Gaylord. Clara and Louise were still playing Queen of the hill. Each acted as if they were in charge of this sinking ship yet neither of them knew how to salvage it, and it was a big surprise to the other one. Clara busted her rump as best she could setting things up and taking care of the DJ and having the cash box and the 50/50 tickets ready and so on. Louise swept in like the Queen of the hop and took over without ever having lifted a finger to do anything. Of course, Clara had her moments too. Listening to that whiney twang of hers was like hearing a seven year old defiantly tell you she was not going to eat her broccoli.

I'm getting a bad reception

If you buy it, they will dance

It was a bright sunny day in October 1996. I had just 'checked in' with the man upstairs at church. I was on my way home and a thought popped into my mind that said 'Go to Sears.' That moment of clarity wasn't exactly the same as 'If you build it, he will come' but it got through to me.

I bought a sound system the way you'd pick up an impulse item at Wal*Mart. In less than 15 minutes I was the proud owner of a Magnavox Home Theatre surround sound stereo. I had no idea what to do with it or why I bought it. It was one of those 'I really had to have it but I don't know why' type of moments. I wasn't really looking for sound equipment. I had so many radios and tape players of all shapes and sizes at home that I could have opened a resale appliance store. I used the new sound system to make rented videos and TV shows sound better. But after awhile, the mighty Magnavox sat gathering dust on the shelf.

Meanwhile, back at the train wreck

Clara wanted to lead the singles group badly, and she did, very badly. Louise would not budge. Louise was a nurse, a supposedly educated woman. After talking to her you would have thought she recently had a lobotomy. Clara had some twenty plus years on Louise. She also had that whiny voice, which reminded me of Bill Dana's character Jose Jimenez.

Clara kept hinting around that she was going to up and take the group to a new and unspecified location that was more affordable than Palmer's. There was also some speculation as to just how long the restaurant was going to stay open for at the time it wasn't doing well.

Clara kept dropping little hints that made it sound like a military coup was at hand. She would mutter little things about the high price of renting the room, which included a waitress and a bartender then not getting either of them once the dances started. That put a sizable bee in Clara's bonnet. The increasingly low turnout at dances and having Louise walk all over her kept that ol' bee a buzzin as well.

Clara had the annoying habit of hinting that she knew something then saying 'I know something but I'm not going to tell you what it is.'

To which I replied 'Then damn it Clara if you DON'T want me to know, DON'T TELL ME!'

By that time, she pretty much saw the writing on the wall as far as the imminent demise of Palmer's Place. She knew but wouldn't tell but acted like she was keeping secrets for the C. I. A. She was exasperating at times.

Gall in the family

On the Sunday night before Christmas 1996 I keeled over in pain and went to the hospital. Usually on Sunday night I was in agony watching Bob Saget on *America's Funniest Home Videos.* However on that night, the pain came from my gall bladder, which was full of little rocks and ready to roll. I had surgery just after New Year 1997 and was off work for two weeks.

One afternoon I was completely bored. I grew tired of watching the decline of Western civilization on the talk show circuit. I played some music on my new sound system. As I was flipping through the tunes, I looked at my sound system and thought 'There must be a way to make this pay for itself.' Soon after that, the idea popped into my head to become a DJ.

I took a dive into the frothy brine of mobile disc jockey entertainment with both feet yet without the slightest clue as to what I was doing. I was blind as a bat named Matt.

I'm getting my group together and taking it on the road

In early 1997, Clara took it upon herself to relocate the singles group and the dances to Grayling, the small town about 25 miles south of Gaylord. The group as we knew it was dead. Clara merely waited for the other shoe to drop before she made the big move.

And then it did.

In early 1997, Palmer's Place closed. It turned out the Palmer's were leasing the building from a Detroit area doctor. The building needed major repairs and big money to bring it up to the Michigan Health Codes. The doctor was using the building as a tax write-off and wasn't interested in pursuing the repairs. It was sad really.

I got the music in me, or maybe its just gas

So there I was. I had a great idea and the right equipment. Yet again I had no clue how to execute my master plan. Plus there was another minor problem, music. Most of the DJ's I've ever seen at dances had great catalogs of music to draw from. They also played the latest in dance mixes, club music, and all the Top 40 material.

I was convinced that my love and knowledge of contemporary music stopped evolving around the same time Tracy Partridge banged out her last note on the tambourine. In 1975 I was a freshman in high school. While everyone else in my school slobbered over the Bay City Rollers and Kiss, I thought The Carpenters were cool, and I still do to this day.

I don't go bar hopping and the 'club' scene in Northern Michigan consists of the Elks and the Eagles. So I thought I was pretty well out of touch with contemporary music. I started buying CD's and tapes hit and miss. I bought songs I liked and thought other people would like as well. I could have been a major stockholder in the Columbia Record Club.

My local library has a collection of CD's of all musical tastes. Over several months I recorded every one I could find onto cassettes. That wasn't easy when you're only allowed to take out three at a time. Rome wasn't built or in this case, taped, in a day.

It has been said that the best laid plans of mice and me, oft gang agley. My big idea of becoming a DJ ganged agley all over me and I really didn't enjoy it.

I came up with a name – *The Music and M.E.* The Music part is self-explanatory. The M.E. stands for Matt Engel, yours truly. I decided to hold a late winter indoor beach party, dance, and picnic. Lots of publicity went out along with a lot of money on my part. Aside from the public service announcements and a local radio spot, one hundred and forty some odd invitations were sent out to everyone I knew in Gaylord. Only a dozen or more odd people, with some people more odd than others, actually showed up. I thought I had

17

dropped the biggest bomb since the one fell on Nagasaki. I thought I was in over my head and had made a colossal mistake.

Clara, let my people go

In the waning days of Palmer's Place, Clara started in on her 'I'm taking my group elsewhere' routine. Apparently several people mentioned in passing how they wanted to keep dancing and keep the group going whether it was in Gaylord or not.

Somewhere in that little pea brain of hers, Clara firmly believed that she could uproot the remnants of the singles club and her loyal legions would follow her to the ends of the earth. It is amazing how somebody that old could be that naïve.

When the dances ended in Gaylord, I pretty much lost contact with Clara and many of the folks I made friends with from the singles club. From various reports, I gathered that the newly relocated singles club was rockin' the house down in Grayling.

Meanwhile, I was busy for several months trying to get started as a DJ. Then, one day after many weeks and months, I got a distress call from the dance hostess with the mostest, Clara herself. Apparently there was trouble in Paradise. With the group's funds diminishing, Clara had to rely on cheaper and cheaper entertainment. At one point I think she was down to either having me be her DJ or playing tissue paper and comb. Now that's entertainment.

2

Breaker breakers

If I was actually going to be a DJ I had to start somewhere. As it turned out, somewhere was a hangout in Grayling called Breakers. By its exotic sounding name, what came to mind was a regal establishment surrounded by waves crashing on the shore with seagulls soaring freely about. What I imagined and what I got were two completely different things entirely. Meanwhile, I was asked to play at a bridal show scheduled for the same day as my very first gig for Clara.

Dear Diary   *March 1, 1997*
It was another typically cold, drizzly day in Gaylord. This was a very busy day for me. It was my first official day as a fully functioning albeit somewhat inexperienced mobile disc jockey. I guess you could call this my baptism by fire. I had two gigs scheduled for the very same day.
The first one was a bridal show at Carters, one of the grocery stores here in Gaylord. My mother, who should also be my agent/receptionist/secretary, arranged this gig for me. She is active

19

in the local Lioness Club and one of the gals who is also in the club works at Carters and was in charge of the bridal show. It really does pay to have connections.

It does not pay to get your signals crossed. There was an ad for an upcoming bridal show. In small letters it said March 1, 1997. In bigger letters it said '11 am– 4 p.m.', someone, either my mother or myself misread it as 11/4, as in November 4th. So I thought I had plenty of time and accepted the gig at Breakers.

It was only a week ago when we realized that it was for TODAY! So this kept me busy. I played 11 a.m. – 4 p.m. at Carters and 8 – Midnight at Breakers.

The bridal show went very well. It was a freebie but the publicity was terrific. It was also the first time many people in Gaylord knew that I was doing anything like this. Many of them asked me if I was still driving the bus. (Since February 9, 1989 I have been a county bus driver for the Otsego County Bus System in Gaylord Michigan.) Of course I am still driving. I wouldn't give that up for anything.

There were two rows of about four or five tables set up with folks sitting in between the rows. My table sat crossways at the end of the two rows. On either side of me were cosmetics demonstrations, cake decorators, crystal stemware demonstrators, as well as limo and tux rental services. I was the sole male and the only DJ there, thank goodness. My sound system faced away from the rest of the tables so as not to drown out the rest of the bridal show participants, or the store itself.

Throughout the afternoon I saw many familiar faces and a few new ones. To my right was an attractive blond in a business suit. She was the wife of a notoriously tough local Michigan State Trouper known as The Terminator. She was a Mary Kay representative at the bridal show.

To my left was a gal I had only seen once before. Her mother was one of the members and eventual presidents of the ill-fated singles club. Her name was Ruby and she had red hair and the volatile disposition that goes along with it. Before Clara, there was Ruby, who likewise sparred with the dimwitted Louise. Louise was the most incredibly clueless person I have ever met.

I'm getting a bad reception

As for Ruby's daughter, she was demonstrating something or other that was wedding related. I didn't recognize her and I was too temporarily clueless as to remember who she was.
'I'm Karlee, you know my mom Ruby, she's the bitch!'
Those were her exact words. I am not making this up.

Little dump by the freeway

Breakers was a dump. There was a small dining room and a bar in the front and a larger room with a dance floor in the back. I was just starting out as a DJ and my sound equipment was a home stereo, which of course, wasn't loud enough for the big room that I was playing. So of course there were problems.

One of them was that the people who were sitting in the bar up front kept complaining that my music wasn't loud enough and they couldn't hear it. I was only supposed to play for the singles in the back, in a separate room no less. The people in the bar had not paid the five bucks to get into the dance but wanted to hear my music just the same. Clara was getting pressure from the people up front and was trying to please both groups unsuccessfully. I was only there to play for the singles, not the barfly's. This situation got ugly fast.

As it was, the attendance at the dances fell off immediately once the curiosity about the new location faded. There were fewer and fewer people showing up each week. For all of her bravado, Clara did not know how to run a group, and basically did not know what she was doing. She managed to take the last fleeting remnants of our singles group and run them into the ground,

The room where the dances were held was right next to the kitchen. The cooks cranked up their kitchen radio louder and louder each week. In the bar, they cranked up the jukebox while I was playing music for the singles. It was a bad situation. Clara started in again with her infantile whispering and chitchat, hinting that the group was moving to some bar further down the highway toward the small town of Mio. If it had moved any further east it would have been in the middle of Lake Huron.

I had had enough. I wrote her a letter and told her off and quit as her DJ. She was in over her head and didn't know her ass from her elbow. But she got what she wanted. She was in charge of whatever this mess of a group was called.

In the meantime:

Palmer's Place remained closed and was eventually torn down. Clara and her tribe vanished and there was no singles club in Gaylord for a long long time.

Some time passed and I had a visit from Melvin, the 50 something friend of my sister. He told me that a few weeks prior to his visit, he saw Clara and that she was quite active with the singles club in Houghton Lake, a resort town about 50 miles south of Gaylord. In fact he told me, Clara moved there years ago to be closer to the singles group. That was a group that was quite popular and alive and active and one that she had not yet destroyed.

Last tango at the Holiday Inn

A few years ago, in 2002 or 2003, yet another feeble attempt was made to have a singles club in Gaylord. A lady who knows my mother, created the Alpine Singles. The lady and her friend created this latest incarnation of a singles club that was an upscale version of what we had. The lady was newly separated from her husband. Her husband met somebody else online and ran off with her. It turned out that his 'greener pasture' was an old friend whom he went to school with many moons before, give or take a moon. The lady with the singles club decided, to paraphrase Mickey and Judy, 'Hey kids, let's put on a singles club.'

Originally, this new lady was considering me to be her DJ. I had a few heated discussions with her right out of the gate. She wanted her group to be for people 45 years old and up. I suggested that she lower the age range to 21 and up like our group was. She informed me that nobody wanted to dance with a 21 year old. I was in my early 30's in the first singles club and always found a dance partner. Her lady friend was feeding her some bad advice and they both fought me tooth and nail on several different issues. And as it turned out, I wasn't even old enough to be in her group since at the time I was a mere lad of 42. I was three years shy of her precious age limit.

I was open and straight up honest with her and warned her of the pitfalls and traps we encountered in our singles group. I warned her of the nitpicking and the hostility as well as the dissention and frustration. She wouldn't listen to a single word I had to say. She informed me that her group would not be like that and that I did not know what I was talking about. I had been through all of this and I sure as hell knew EXACTLY what I talking about. I got fed up and emailed her, told her off and suggested she find another DJ and that I did not need this aggravation.

The new group had a few dances. I think there was, a grand total of two, which they shelled out a king's ransom for, to put on at the Holiday Inn. Those dances were a lot more lavish than the crackers and cheese and Chicken Dance affairs that our group put on.

The new group did a few other things but started to deteriorate faster than ours did. The ditzy woman in charge of it was quoted in the local paper as 'basking in the afterglow of one successful dance.' I don't know how long she basked because her wandering husband came back to her with his tail between his legs and so the dancing queen took him back. Soon after the great romance of the new millennium was reconciled, they moved away.

The new group had more dances but they had them all over town. I think the last one was held at a local golf course/country club called Michaywe`. The group, which had been the melba toast of the town at the Holiday Inn, was quickly running out of money and was being charged an arm and a leg to hold a dance in a room at the Michaywe` clubhouse. The group was charging six dollars a piece to get into their dance and that did not even include drinks, which added up quickly even with soft drinks.

I went to one of their dances because one of the gals who was in charge of the group, or had it dumped in her lap by the basking dancing queen, was interested in having me be the DJ for the group. It was déjà vu. Melvin was there; Clara was there with her Houghton Lake posse to give the new group the once over. Clara had an attitude the size of Montana by then. Apparently she was the Queen of the Hop down in Houghton Lake, big deal.

I'm getting a bad reception

The new group was frightfully dull. Their DJ was a lady who had been a fixture in the Houghton Lake group for some time and Clara was one of her groupies. I had a dance, two very expensive Diet Cokes and left after an hour. I knew I could have played just as well as she did, and a friend in the group tried valiantly about six times to get them cooperate and hire me to play for them. The members of the group could not have cared less about me if they tried.

In June of 2003, at the suggestion of another friend from Louise's group, I attended a meeting of what was left of this latest incarnation of a singles group. I went to the meeting and it was creepy. It was the same old bickering and crap only played out with different people. It was as if they took a long running television series and recast every role with new people for no reason. There was a Clara character, a Louise character. It was like watching a bad play. I typed out a nice resume, told those people that I would work with them on developing the group, running the dances, publicity, whatever they wanted I would help them with. I never heard from them again.

Every so often there is a blurb about the group in the local paper listed under Activities. I have a pretty good hunch that this was one of those public service announcements that they put in the paper ages ago and no one ever called to tell them to remove it. There was a Commodore Computer Users Group that used to have meetings but disbanded, but the P. S. A. ran long after Commodore Computers went out of business. For a while there was even an announcement for the monthly Jaycee meetings and at that time, Gaylord had not had a Jaycee Chapter for several years. Out of morbid curiosity I am tempted to call the number for the singles club to see if they are still active, but I highly doubt they are.

Of course I could always call Clara.

Not!

3

My first wedding:
My baby and me and Stanley make three

My first wedding reception took place, oddly enough, just about a mile from Breakers. It was at the Eagles club in Grayling Michigan. The hall sits next to southbound I-75 on highway M-72 headed east out of town. Breakers, in its dumpy splendor, sat on the other side of the freeway in an air industrial park.

The bride wrote me a list of the songs she wanted and it was exciting to see everything coming together for this very first big wedding. It is an odd thing to get excited about I know but it felt like making contact with a different life form. Over the years I have learned that many of my brides and some of my grooms seem like a different life form altogether. As for getting excited about something so minor, in the early 1970's when I saw my very first Xerox machine at the public library I thought it was the greatest thing since sliced bread. It was brand new technology without carbon paper and it was amazing to me at the time. Either that or I really needed to get out more.

I'm getting a bad reception

That first party in Grayling began my history of playing weddings, it likewise continued my tradition of shopping for music that I didn't already have. I started keeping a list, which became a full catalog of every song I have in my collection. This has been a valuable tool for me on many levels. Mainly it lets me know exactly what music I have as well as being a quick reference guide for looking up songs for customers when they bombard me with requests. Next, it serves as a kind of 'get away from me kid you bother me' diversion when invariably some guest will wander over to me after four hours of playing and ask me 'What kind of music do you have?' I gladly hand them my songbook and they'll take it off to one side of the room and look for songs they want to hear. It gets them off my back for awhile and when people start gathering around the book, they pour over it and scrutinize it like a pack of wolves about to devour fresh kill. In the beginning my collection was small and I used to send each customer a copy of my songbook along with an information packet and an informal agreement. Presently the songbook is nearing 300 pages and I don't send it out anymore.

Artist and song are displayed in the songbook in alphabetical order to save myself a long drawn out treasure hunt each time I get a request. I also list the album it is on, the disc as well as the track number. I once had a very dear friend tell me that since I am a Virgo I am meticulous. That is definitely the case and it has come in handy over the years. It is not so ridiculous being meticulous.

The following is an example of a listing in my songbook.

BEACH BOYS (Pop)	Album name	Location
All summer long	American Graffiti Soundtrack	Disc 2 – Track 20

I have molded, shaped, sculpted, primped and pruned this songbook over the years. My CD's are stored in their carrying cases in alphabetical order. I have made my own labels for every disc and the songs are listed in red and blue lettering. Red indicates a fast song, blue indicates a slow song, and songs with an asterisk before and after the title and in italics are great to dance to.

My songbook has been in black and white since the beginning and I am gradually changing it to color to match the labels. The book is definitely a work in progress. I think of it like one of those European cathedrals they began building back in the 1500's and still haven't finished yet. Talk about procrastination.

For my first wedding the bride wanted me to play *When you say nothing at all* by Allison Krauss. It is a beautiful song but I did not have it so I bought it on cassette. I don't mind buying the music especially if it is by an artist as talented as Allison Krauss. Over the years I have acquired a lot of good music, much of it lately on I – Tunes and at bargain basement prices on Amazon.com. Occasionally I have even had couples record their own favorite music on a disc to have me to play it at the party if I don't have it in the catalog, which is fine with me too. This saves me the wear and tear on my CD's and makes the customer happy so it all works out.

The groom for that very first wedding called me and unbeknownst to his bride-to-be wanted my help in planning a special surprise for her at the reception. He wanted to know if I had the song *I cross my heart* by George Strait. He was going to sing it for his bride at the reception. I soon found the song and I knew it was going to be one of the special moments of the night. I don't have karaoke equipment, which is even more excess baggage to lug around. I have seriously considered several times over the years, investing in a semi truck just to play at parties. To solve the karaoke problem I would play the song low enough to hear the music then crank up the microphone for the groom's serenade.

To get ready for the party I packed bag and baggage into my car. Any more equipment stuffed into my vehicle and people passing me on the road would have only seen two eyeballs peering out at them from inside the car as I drove by.

I was nervous with anticipation leading up to that party. The nervousness increased on the way down to the gig and I was close to catatonic by the time I got to the hall. I had flop sweat like a sumo wrestler. The hall was already getting crowded and I think my knees were buckling. I have been on stage many times in plays and skits and have spoken many times at church but I always get stage fright before I go on. That first wedding reception was a trip through uncharted waters for me. Walking into a crowd and setting up my equipment was like building the sets for a play just as the audience is taking their seats in a theatre.

There was a stage in the opposite corner from the main door that was about three and a half to four feet high. I honed in on the stage right away. I decided to set up shop on the bingo stage of the Eagles hall. On the wall above the stage was an electric sign with Bingo numbers streaming out from each letter. Those numbers lit up as they were called. There was a table and a collection of other odds and ends of Bingo equipment covered up with sheets.

I set up my catch as catch can sound system on the table and set up my speakers wherever there was room. I was not thinking clearly that night and only later noticed that directly across the hall from me was a wide open dance floor as well as a long wooden table that sat by its lonesome all night waiting for me. It didn't register that I was actually supposed to be by the dance floor instead of hovering over the crowd in a corner like a condor guarding its nest. There was a comfortable office chair on the stage which felt a lot better than the metal chairs that were sprinkled throughout the room, so that is where I stayed all night.

Directly beneath the stage and to my right was the head table wedged into a corner between the stage and the nearest wall. Along the wall was a side door, which I eventually pulled up to and parked by, and that was where I unloaded my 'toys.' Over the years I have come to know the location of every service entrance, kitchen door and loading dock of every hall within a thirty-mile radius. It helps to have this inside information.

Fanning out from the head table were the tables for the guests. At the table closest to the head table and directly in front of me were two ladies. One of them looked at my sound equipment, then looked to each other and one of them sniffed 'Is that ALL that he has?' Referring to my DJ setup. At least that is what I HOPE she was referring to. That question came up a lot amongst the guests when I first started out. People assumed that since I had a smaller sound system I was somehow less of a DJ. Happily I have proven most of the naysayers wrong.

I had not been to a wedding as a guest in a long time prior to this. I had forgotten about the joy of little children at such events. There is more on this subject later in this book. The bridal party had several assorted little rug rats among them. I was glad I was a little higher up

28

than the screaming banshees. They could have been dangerous at ground level.

I got a little, nay, a lot more nervous when unloading my stock of CD's and sound equipment. I could not find one of the bags that held about a third of my CD's and tapes. I made a frantic call home thinking I might have left it behind. No such luck, it was not there. I had to turn down a lot of requests because those songs were on the discs I had forgotten at home.

I don't remember what song I played to start that first wedding. I don't even remember playing dinner music. I will however never forget playing the bride and groom's first song. I made the announcement for them to come to the floor, a custom that I have long since written down as opposed to winging it on the microphone. It sounds more professional when it is recited than improvised. The first dance was very romantic and the crowd was properly respectful, reflective and caught up in the moment.

The rest of the formal dances came and went without a hitch. Then came the big moment of the night, the groom's secret serenade to his bride. The groom came up to the stage and called for his bride. The bridesmaids must have been in on it because the bride was surrounded by maroon taffeta dresses on both sides as far as the eye could see. The bridesmaids to the immediate right and left of the bride were locked arm in arm with the unsuspecting bride. I think they held a death grip on her to keep her from fainting from the emotion of the moment, or turning and running out the door.

The song began, the groom sang quite well as if he were George Strait himself. There were tears flowing like a fine wine. There were tears in the groom's eye, the bridesmaids, the guests and mine. The bride was overcome and looked like she was going to crash to the floor any second. It was a very touching, tender moment. I was caught up in the moment and so relieved that everything was going so well I got a little emotional myself. The song was a hit.

George Strait starred in the movie *Pure Country* many years ago. At the end of the movie he sings *I cross my heart* in the showroom at the Mirage in Las Vegas. He sings it face to face to a cowgirl named Harley (actress Isabel Glasser) whom he has fallen in love with. It is the big emotional, lump in the throat moment at the end of the film.

I'm getting a bad reception

There was not a dry eye in the house. Same song, same reaction at the Eagles hall in Grayling as there was in Las Vegas.

During a break I went over to the kitchen and got something to eat. I have had the best food at weddings. That has been one of the perks of being a DJ, more on this subject also later in the book. I had a plate full of food and I wandered into the kitchen looking for something, perhaps silverware, a cup, sedatives, I forget exactly what. There was an older gal in the kitchen straightening things out, putting things away, etc.

I said 'Excuse me ma'am, are you the mother of the bride?'

She said 'Oh goodness no my dear, I am her grandmother.'

I said 'Well you sure don't look old enough to be a grandmother.'

She smiled and thanked me and complimented me on the nice job I was doing with the music. That was a great moment and I needed that.

After the cake and the bouquet and the garter, it was time to get rocking. Right around seven or seven thirty I noticed that my audience was quickly diminishing. Good Lord, I thought, I didn't think I was playing THAT bad! Well it wasn't me who caused this exodus, it was a chap named Stanley.

The night of June 7, 1997 was the deciding game of a four game Stanley Cup playoff series between The Detroit Red Wings and the Philadelphia Flyers. As the game progressed people went home to watch it. I should have been clued into this because one lady came to the reception dressed in sneakers, white shorts and a bright red and white Red Wings jersey. I was taken aback by such informality at a wedding. That outfit is tame now compared to what I have seen walking into receptions over the years. It is amazing how many people must shop at the '*I don't give a damn what I look like when I go out in public*' store at their local mall. I am no fashion expert myself but there is a time and place for everything.

There were TV's mounted in every corner of the room that would have normally been used for Bingo. If the dance portion of the evening got dull I thought I could always crank up the Bingo ball tumbler and call a few numbers.

I'm getting a bad reception

Throughout the hall, the TV sets were turned to the hockey game. People rapidly became less interested in the wedding and dancing and more interested in the Red Wings quest for Lord Stanley's cup.

Long about eight or eight-thirty it was all over but the shouting. The few hangers on could not have cared less about the wedding and were all parked in front of the TV sets. Many or most of them stood in front of the screen that hung directly to the left of the Bingo stage. I was on a roll with the music so I was in no hurry to leave. The crowd got smaller by the minute. Most of those in attendance went home to catch the game. There was also a large crowd gathered in the bar of the Eagles club to watch the game as well.

I wasn't sure what to play so I just went willy-nilly through the collection playing a little bit of this and that. People had been throwing raw octopi (see: octopus) onto the ice during Red Wings games that season. I was not sure why they did so until I found the following on a website called kidzworld.com:

Bizarre sports fan traditions:
Octopus on Ice.

For nearly 50 years, hockey fans in Detroit have been throwing octopi on to the ice after a big win by the Red Wings. This started on April 15, 1952 during the Red Wings' Stanley Cup run. Two brothers, Pete and Jerry Cusimano, who owned a fish shop in Detroit threw an octopus on the ice during a game in Detroit. Each tentacle of the octopus was symbolic of a win in the playoffs. Back then, the NHL had just six teams and eight wins (two best-of-seven series) were needed to win the Stanley Cup. The largest octopus to be thrown on the ice was a 50 pounder in 1996. The creature was proudly displayed on the hood of the Zamboni while the ice at the Joe Louis Arena was being cleaned between periods.

I sure would have hated to have to clean up after them. In light of the octopus bombardment I played *Octopus's Garden* by the Beatles. I was trying to go with the sports atmosphere of the evening so I played *Be true your school* by The Beach Boys.

The Detroit Red Wings won the Stanley Cup that night by beating Philadelphia 2 –1, much to the delight of the remainder of the wedding guests and the rowdy crowd that spilled out of the bar and into the hall. I got hit with a lot of requests all at once. Thankfully I was not hit with any octopi. Most of those requests were for *We are the champions* from Queen. I did not have that song in my collection at the time. The rowdy crowd from the bar pretty much took over the main room of the Eagles hall and my time at that reception was over. And it wasn't even ten o'clock. It is amazing that after all of the preparation and anxiety and effort that went into getting ready for the party, it was over so fast. The bride and groom were quite happy with me and the groom, who was also a DJ, complimented me and said I did a great job. As I was packing up, I found the supposedly missing CD and tape bag tucked into a corner of my car, where it was the whole time.

I survived playing for my first wedding. On the way home I stopped by Breakers and peaked into the window to see how the singles dance was going. Both people who were there seemed to be having a good time.

4

Stop! Hey! What's that sound?

From the earliest days of my DJ experience, all the way back to the bridal show, the debacle that was Breakers, the first wedding and for nearly two years afterward, my DJ sound system was a Magnavox home theatre unit with surround sound. It had two big speakers and two smaller ones. I bought a rotating mirrored ball and made a feeble attempt to shine a weak flashlight on it.

The Magnavox was my receiver and the speakers were plugged in to the back of it. To that I added a home stereo CD player. My library of CD's was still pretty small at the time and I have always been blown away at how good they sound. The days of scratchy LP records were fading into the sunset as new technology and newer and neater toys came to be.

The very first ever CD that I bought was the original London Production of *Phantom of the Opera.* I bought the CD even before I bought a CD player. I took it to my nephew's house and at the first blast of music, in the part of the show where the chandelier rises from the stage and hovers over the audience, the front metal plate fell off the wall heater and hit the floor with a resounding crash. I have loved CD's ever since.

The CD unit for my DJ work had what was known as a magazine. You put in six discs at a time and played them once the magazine has been reinserted. Most of the DJ's that I have seen or heard switch from song to song seamlessly with no break in the music. I hadn't gotten to that point yet. As it was there were noticeable gaps in between songs while changing discs.

My father, who is clever at woodworking, made me a frame on which I hung my light, and presumably any lights I might use in the future. I brought a lot more in the way of props and scenery than I do now. I used to have this four-foot high cardboard cutout of a jukebox that I would attach to the front of the table where my equipment sat. I attached it to the wall behind me surrounded by large black plastic musical notes and a bass clef. I was compensating for a lack of equipment. (There is a dirty joke in there somewhere but I'll leave it to the reader to find it.) The next feature I added to my ensemble was a dual tape deck.

Using music on tape for dances was primitive to say the least. It is nearly impossible to find music and cue it up properly unless you set the timer to zero and the tape back to the beginning and mark down the numbers as they change for each track. I had most of my local library's CD collection on cassette by that time. The Internet was still new and we had dial up at the house so downloading and recording music online was still foreign to me. I think I was still using an out of date Macintosh Performa Computer, or perhaps it was even a Fisher Price XP at the time.

But hey, I had to start somewhere and I think I did okay with what I had. I have seen DJ's with far more expensive equipment, music and accessories than I had. DJ equipment is not cheap so I got what I could get when I could get it. Again, there is a dirty joke in there.

I have seen some DJ's with enough concert lighting, sound mixers and amplifiers to cover a Rolling Stones tour. I have seen towers of lights and boxes of sound equipment and speakers so big and loud you could hear them twenty miles away. That is all well and good but I am just one guy who has to lug all that heavy equipment around by himself. I have a bad back that I am trying to keep in tact so I had to figure out how to get my act together and take it on the road and keep myself in one piece.

I'll get back to my back later. The story of which will send chills up your spine, no bones about it.

From time to time, DJ's have to make announcements so the next piece of equipment for my arsenal was a microphone. I plugged the microphone into a heavy guitar amp that I think weighed as much as my first car. It was cumbersome and the microphone was not very powerful but short of yelling at the top of my lungs all night, it did the job.

I knew there had to be more to being a wedding DJ than my piecemeal attempt at it. I bought a book called *The Mobile Dj Handbook: How to Start and Run a Profitable Mobile Disc Jockey Service* by Stacy Zemon (Butterworth-Heinemann - June 1997). The book laid it on the line and explained most everything I needed to know about being a 'mobile DJ.' I had never heard the term 'mobile DJ'. For all I knew a 'mobile' DJ was somebody from Alabama. I had a lot to learn.

The book covered a wide range of topics and was invaluable to me. It covered everything from being a club DJ to playing at weddings.

The book went on to explain what I would need as far as equipment and music. It described how to play music based on beats per minute and what every DJ should wear to a party. I tend to go more with the number of dancers on the floor and what they are responding to rather than beat per minute. As for DJ fashion, apparently many DJ's wear a suit or a tuxedo. I have never worn a tuxedo because if I wore one I would look an over stuffed penguin, and a suit is not my long suit. I go Sunday casual at most parties. A sweater and church slacks and nice shoes when it is cooler. I wear the same outfit minus the sweater and a nice polo shirt in the summer. I figure that the guests do not come to look at me; they come to dance and party. I would rather they dance and party to my music all night than look at me and laugh or run away screaming.

The book suggested that some DJ's get out on the floor and really whip the crowd into a frenzy. I have seen video of some DJ's wearing funny hats, shaking maracas and leading a conga line. When I first started as a DJ I was already bringing enough props and scenery and equipment to stage a production of *My fair lady*. The thought of lugging any more did not thrill me at all.

The music is what the people want. And that is what I give them. The music and me, that is it, no frills. And that is how I came up with my DJ name. As explained in Chapter One, the music is self-explanatory; the M. E. is my initials Matt Engel. I was going to call myself the New York Philharmonic or the London Symphony Orchestra but those names were already taken.

I had a potential customer recently who seemed overly concerned about his guests. He had it in mind that I should go table to table and entertain as if I were Adam Sandler in *The Wedding Singer*. I don't do that. I don't travel the room making small talk and DJ patter. I work the sound system and spin the platters. Now if I had someone working with me it would be a different story altogether. But it is just me over there in the corner behind the sound system. When the potential customer called me I had a hunch he was going to be trouble right out of the box. His attitude answered the phone ten minutes before he did.

'Well I don't want to have to walk from table to table all night making sure my guests are happy.' He informed me on the phone in a voice that made him sound like he was 14.

Well neither do I, I thought. I replied to him in a nice long letter in which I basically told him what was what and suggested he find another DJ. Needless to say I never heard from him again. No big loss.

Another revelation I discovered in the (helpful beyond words) DJ book was the concept of a written agreement between my potential customers and myself. It was your basic 'What do you want me to do and when do I do it?' type of agreement.

To help the potential customers get to know me better I added bits and pieces to the initial contract. Over the years this has evolved into the DJ information packet, some of which I have re-created in the Appendix in the back of this book on page 154.

One big lesson I learned early on was to keep in touch with the customers otherwise they will think you went the way of Jimmy Hoffa or Amelia Erhart. In the beginning I would make first contact and not respond right away, for no other reason than procrastination.

I'm getting a bad reception

There was a case where a potential customer who lived near Ann Arbor, was going to have a wedding at her parents home on the Ausable River in Grayling. It was going to be an all day blowout divided into several segments. There was going to be a meet and greet then the 'I do's' and a short trip in a tippy canoe (and Tyler too!) It was either going to be a canoe trip or a cross-country drive or a caravan of some kind. Then it was back to the starting point for dinner and what have you. By the way, I do not charge extra for what have you.

The bride to be (or not to be) called me on the phone, she talked in the clench jawed manor of Jim Backus from *Gilligan's Island* mixed with Miss Hathaway from *The Beverly Hillbillies*. I was hoping that during our short phone conversation she would either say 'Oh Lovey' or 'Oh Mr. Drysdale.' But she didn't.

She told me on the phone that she and her intended had a few special songs that they wanted me to play for the reception. I vaguely remember but I think they wanted me to play for the ceremony as well. She most likely wanted me in the bow of the canoe so if anything happened I would be the first to go, like the steerage passengers on the Titanic. I was still new at the DJ game and I did not have the extensive library of music I have today. I also did not have access to the Internet and its vast surplus of downloadable music. On the other hand I did not have a good excuse for taking so long to get back to her either. By the time I did, she wrote me the following letter.

> *I received your letter the end of last week regarding the 2 songs we are interested in. I am very concerned about the time frame it took for you to respond to my questions. Three weeks is a long time considering you have my home phone number (Voice Mail), pager number thru the voice mail message, email.*
>
> *My financee (sic) and I have discussed this concern. Our wedding day is very special to the both of us. We want people there that are committed to our day. Taking three weeks to receive a simple response from you does not indicate that*

37

commitment to us. Thank you for your time but we have decided to look into other DJ services for our wedding.

Okay, lesson learned, I blew it. These days I respond immediately, not weeks or months. Or is that moths? However in my own feeble defense, when I got around to responding she was nearly impossible to track down. I tried everything short of sending up smoke signals and a carrier pigeon in order to get in touch with her. And I responded in kind.

The last time I heard from you was by email. In that very same email you said you had received my paperwork and would be filling it out and would send my check to me as soon as you could. You indicated in that email that your fiancé hadn't gotten the names of his groomsmen together yet and when he did I'd receive my paperwork and check. I hadn't heard from you in nearly a month and I figured you were still working on the paperwork. I was waiting for you to send my paperwork back and it's been some time now and you never sent it back. I figured you needed some time so I held back and did not respond right away.

I take great exception to the fact that in your recent email you said I lacked the commitment to be a part of your special day. When plans for this reception were first made I called all over southern Lower Michigan to get in touch with you. I talked to a machine, a pager and eventually someone who works for you and finally I talked to you on the phone. To be fair you are not the easiest person in the world to get in touch with, regardless of the wonders of modern technology that are readily available these days.

When we talked on the phone we discussed the preliminary plans for the wedding and eventually I sent you my paperwork, the whole nine yards. I sent you my perpetually updated songbook. A few weeks ago I sent you a page full of updates and additions to my song list. You responded with an email saying I didn't have two songs you wanted. I also mentioned that I would be sending you my complete list of songs on CD and cassette for even more choices. And then I get an email from you stating that since you hadn't heard from me in 3 weeks, I apparently don't care about your wedding and you are going to find somebody else to play for you. I feel I have kept in very close contact with you and to just drop me like that is totally unfair. But it is your decision and your money and you may spend it however you wish.

Further regarding my commitment to your wedding reception, I think you should likewise know that I have gone out and bought music on a weekly basis to perk up the catalog, including two CD's of Clint Black and Lonestar. I have likewise spent several hundred dollars on new equipment to provide a better variety of music for you and your guests. I have been pricing new speakers and a soundboard in order to make your party even better. Now if I really didn't want to be a part of your party I would have waltzed down to Grayling with poor equipment and a poor music selection. So your accusation that I am not committed to your 'special day' is out of line and unfair.

I apologize for the gruff nature of this letter but in light of your abrupt decision to seek another DJ, threw me for a loop and I didn't know how else to respond. I think you will be hard pressed to find someone to play for you at the price I ask at this late date. I'm sure you will have a great day and great entertainment. On my part it may take awhile to recoup all the money I have shelled out in recent weeks buying things for your wedding, which I won't be playing for now. Once again I apologize for the terse, gruff and sarcastic nature of this letter but in light of recent events I feel I had no other choice.

Best wishes for your wedding.

Matt Engel

Gee, I can't understand why I never heard from her again.

On the other side of the coin there have been a few occasions where I have received the initial call to play at a party and have mailed the customer my information packet and I never hear from them again. It is as if they have vanished off the face of the earth. There was even a case where a potential customer wanted to meet me so I picked a nice restaurant downtown and a time to meet. I was there at the appropriate time with contract and sample music discs in hand. An hour or so went by and I sat there watching my over priced cream of mushroom soup harden into concrete. The mystery customer never showed up and to this day I have no idea what happened to her.

Oh well, win some, lose some, lesson learned. It pays to R. S. V. P. - A. S. A. P. or I will be S. O.L., you see?

Sometimes I wonder whatever happens to the couples I have played for over the years. I have seen a few of them around town from time to time but most of them have vanished from my radar.

I know that a few of them have even gotten divorced. It is a shame when your wedding ceremony and reception lasts longer that your marriage. I have jokingly considered putting a divorce clause in my agreement stating 'If you get a divorce, you don't get your money back.'

5

Dread of the class – or –
Reunited and I feel so annoyed

Aside from the occasional odd wedding, and as you will read, some are more odd than others; I have played a few high school class reunions. Unless you actually know someone in the class you are playing for, or are in the class yourself, reunions can be a lonely night. To me a reunion is a free flowing event that is not nearly as neatly structured as a wedding and a reception.

For the most part I feel that I am merely a decoration in the background at a reunion. I would probably feel that way at my own class reunion as well, let alone someone else's. Unless there are a lot of events scheduled during the party there is dinner and drinking and talking and some guy playing in the corner, and that would be me.

I have only played three class reunions and more than likely will never play another one. At reunions people are more comfortable sitting and chatting with old friends than they are shaking their booty out on the floor. All three of the reunions were for the two high schools in Gaylord. Two of them were for Gaylord High School, class of 1967 and 1972 respectively. The other reunion was for the St.

I'm getting a bad reception

Mary's Catholic High School, class of 2002. The first two reunions took place within a few weeks of each other.

Hidden Valley Resort, Gaylord Michigan

The class of '67 met in the beautiful main dining room of Hidden Valley Resort in Gaylord. The resort has a vintage up north look and is very homey. There is skiing, golf, dining, the whole nine yards as well as the whole 18 holes. Big picture windows throughout the main lodge give you a great view especially in the autumn when Mother Nature puts on a dazzling display of color.

The main lodge of the resort has two dining rooms, The Sitz Mark, on the west end has a long wooden fully stocked bar, The Headwaters Dining Room is on the east end. The Headwaters is a formal dining room that I could never in three lifetimes afford to eat in. In between the two dining rooms is a comfortable lobby

The class of '67 reunion was in the Headwaters room. You walked in to the room and saw several elegantly appointed tables surrounding a small dance floor. On the other side of the dance floor and along the wall, was yours truly.

I had no clue what kind of music to play. This was the class of 1967, the summer of love. What could they possibly want to hear? Hendrix? The Beatles? Something from *Sgt. Pepper's Lonely Hearts Club Band?* They were 30 years older and out of high school. Did they want Jazz? Swing? Gregorian Chant? As it turned out they were not paying a great deal of attention to me anyway so it didn't matter.

Looking out over the sea of strange faces I had a lot of time to kill and tried to imagine who among those with the crow's feet and middle aged spread were the hippies, the rebels, the brains, the jocks and the others. At one point I cut the music and those in attendance gave a brief history of their lives since high school. They commented about absent friends, those who simply did not show up and people with whom they had lost contact over the years. Other friends, those who had passed on were mentioned as well. One or two of their classmates gave their lives for their country in Vietnam. Some came back and left part of themselves over there. There was one guy, husky, graying, wire rim glasses, who was a party animal in school, I

42

feared he might reprise that role that night. He turned out to have quit drinking years ago and was one of the first people to leave the party. The reunion was a learning experience as well being somewhat somber and morose.

One rather humorous incident that sticks out in my mind was with this longhaired brunette in a long blue denim dress. She was either the spouse of a classmate or a classmate herself. She and her husband were members of a large Baptist church here in Gaylord.

The woman and her husband chatted with a group of friends on the other side of the room. She broke free from the chitchat and crossed the room to talk to me. We talked for a few minutes as I sifted through my music to determine what I would play next. She asked me the usual questions such as 'How long have you been a DJ?'

'A few years' I told her, and also that in real life I was a local Dial-a-Ride driver.

'Oh, so how long have you been doing that?'

'Since February 9, 1989.'

Then she asked how long I had lived in Gaylord Michigan.

'Since May of 1986'

Then she asked me if I had accepted Jesus Christ as my personal Savior.

'Yes I had.' I replied. 'Years ago.'

'Exactly when did you find Jesus?'

With all of my being I wanted to blurt out, I didn't know He was missing. But I refrained. I nearly bit off my tongue but I was nice. I don't feel that I should have to roll out my church resume` as if I were applying for a job. I am indeed a Christian. There are times however when I am not very good at it. But I believe in a loving, forgiving Lord and Savior who knows everything about me and loves me anyway. He is the ultimate best friend.

The woman asked me what kind of music I play and much to my surprise she wanted to hear a song, *Top of the world,* by the Carpenters. I have been a lifelong fan of the Carpenters so I was happy to oblige her request. The woman told me that she used to like rock and roll music before she became a Christian.

'I used to "get down" once in awhile,' to quote old 1960's slang for dancing. 'That was before I became born again and had six kids.'

I thought, well you must have gotten down, maybe even up and down, more than once if you have six kids running around. I thought I would need surgery to reattach my tongue because I was close to biting it off, but I controlled myself.

It is amazing to me that people can still equate rock and roll music with evil. Some secular music is great and I would never call Bruce Springsteen or Bob Seger or The Beatles evil. I'm sure even Ozzy Osbourne has some forgivable qualities. Although he mumbles so much you can never really understand what those qualities are, but you see my point. Music and dancing are not evil. Did we learn nothing from *Footloose*?

Toward the shank of the evening, and this party shanked earlier than others, the crowd dwindled down to a precious few. I was moments away from tearing down and packing up (or was that cracking up?) when a fermented Fred and Ginger Wannabee discovered that I was in the room after all those hours of playing and had a lot of requests, many that I had already played, as well as a lot of liquor inside them.

I played their requests as best I could. They did their little dance, shook their groove thing and waltzed off into the night.

Class of 1972

The Oak Room, Treetops Sylvan Resort, Gaylord, Michigan

Not much to tell really, a low turn out at best. The Oak Room sits at the top of a seemingly endless, mile high, staircase. It may have been the stairway to Heaven and I figured that if there were a few more steps I was actually going to be in Heaven. I have heard of another DJ who charged one hundred dollars extra because he had to climb the stairs.

I still had my home stereo and acoustically the room was awful. It had a pointed, cathedral ceiling and I think the notes of music I played that night went up into the ceiling and never came back down. They might still be up there today.

Other than the acoustics, the room was beautiful. It had a full service kitchen that rivaled a four star restaurant. I searched every nook and cranny in the kitchen for any sign of a service elevator so I did not have to scale Mt. Everest with my equipment when it was time to go, but no such luck.

The Magnavox gave it the old college try but the alumni could barely hear me. I could have placed my sound system smack dab in the middle of every table with my speakers strapped to people's faces and they still would not have heard me. It did not help that the guests were on the other side of the room, making it seem as if I were three counties away.

Again as it turned out, this was a night made more for chatting than dancing. The lady who hired me, whom I knew from the singles club, wanted me to fire up the crowd. This group of her classmates would not have been fired up with a flamethrower and a can of unleaded gasoline.

Toward the end of the party, some of the small crowd left, a few others danced, some wanted to hear songs from their graduation year of 1972, and I happily obliged.

Our Lady of the wooden ruler across your knuckles
Class of 1982

Hidden Valley Resort, Gaylord Michigan

In July 2002 I played what would be my last class reunion, which was for the alumni of St. Mary's Catholic High School in Gaylord. Oddly enough it was in the same building as the Class of 1967, only in the Sitz Mark Room at the opposite end of the building. Again the décor of this building is very cozy Northern Michigan Lodge with lots of wood everywhere and comfortable furniture and deep blue carpeting.

I had been in that room a few times before, as well as the Headwaters Room. In 1993 I played Henry, the old actor in a local presentation of *The Fantasticks!* In the Sitz Mark Room I had performed in a local talent show called *Sunday Nite Live.* Three guesses as to which late night institution was ripped off for that show. As I have been doing since high school, I wrote and performed my own version of *Weekend Update News.* It went over quite well. This was the Gaylord Area Council for the Arts annual talent show. In describing them, picture the Stepford Wives in sweaters and pageboy haircuts and lots of people who use the phrase 'Oh how fun!' and that should paint a pretty picture with words for you.

I was in the show twice, first with Weekend Update, than later I was put in costume and makeup for a scene called *Samurai Conductor.* If he had not already been doing so, I am sure John Belushi was rolling over in his grave at my portrayal of his famous character leading a symphony orchestra. The nadir of the evening however was when a local bar owner got up and did a liquor fueled stand up comedy routine in which he told everyone on the Arts Council to kiss his ass. My two routines were *Masterpiece Theatre* compared to that.

Meanwhile, back at the Class of 1982 reunion:

It was a beautiful, warm sunny day in July 2002 when I set up shop in the Sitz Mark room. By the time the reunion rolled around I had lived in Gaylord for 16 years and thought I might know some of the alumni. I saw their class photo and nametags and some were recognizable but none of those that I recognized showed up for the reunion.

The hours went by and the room slowly swelled with alumni. I put on some Kenny G for background music until things got hopping later. Kenny G and cocktails and conversation worked pretty well for a while.

One of the alumni was this nerdy, Poindexter looking character with glasses, pursed lips, scrunchy face and peepsy little glasses, who was probably the audio visual guy in school. The guy who wheeled the creaky old movie projector into your third hour science class so you could watch '*Your esophagus and you.*'

After a good run of Kenny G, Poindexter slithers over to me and says 'Don't you have any faster music? We're not OLD you know?'

Yeah, well, excuse me all to hell Nerdzilla!

I bumped up the music and it got louder through cocktails. The music was loud enough at dinner to drown out everyone's dinner conversation but the guests did not seem to mind. I threw the best music I had at them. There were a few times when I was tempted to throw something ELSE at them, like a large rock or a right cross to the mouth.

I'm getting a bad reception

By the time I did that party I had invested in some new DJ equipment (more on that later), some of which I was still shaky on how to use. That particular night I was having some technical problems with my new microphone and every so often I would get this ear piercing feedback coming through the speakers. Poindexter made it a point to waddle over and make snide comments to me.

'Listen I'm sorry about the technical problems on the microphones tonight. Some of this stuff is still new to me.' I said, in a rather friendly, casual way.

He sniffed 'Well if you knew what you were doing you wouldn't have those problems would you?'

I thought, Yeah well bite me, you condescending, beady eyed little twerp, but I did not say it.

It struck me as sad that this was the graduating class from a local Catholic school yet they acted as if they had just escaped from reform school. Before dinner someone suggested that a blessing be said before dinner. I figured 'Oh there is hope yet.' A room full of one hundred or so supposedly mature adults morphed into a class of bratty, sarcastic third graders who recited the following with all the attitude and snide countenance of Simon Cowell from *American Idol*:

> God is great
> God is good
> And we thank Him for this food.
> Amen.

There was absolutely no reverence or respect to be found anywhere near that blessing. It dawned on me that many of those people were most likely sent to Catholic School because they were too obnoxious and rowdy for public school and their parents wanted to straighten them out. Where was that hot tempered nun with the ruler and the rosary beads when you needed her.

After dinner the music stopped and one by one the alumni came up to the microphone and shared the story of their lives with the crowd. It was the same story about lives, wives, husbands, family, kids career, etc. After 'story hour' there was a slide show which everyone seemed to enjoy. There was a projector and a screen set up, probably by Poindexter. It was requested that I play *Dream on* by Aerosmith during the presentation.

When it was finally time to crank up the music and dance I was instantly bombarded with requests. Most of the requests were for heavy metal hair bands from the 1980's, many of which I had never heard of and did not have in my collection at the time. There were cocktail napkins scrawled with requests piled up on the table in front of me like food orders in the kitchen of a greasy spoon. I knew that I would never get to most of these requests even if I had every song they wanted. If I played every song on those napkins the party would have lasted five days. But I did the best I could with what I had.

Another alumnus was a tall skinny, bald, menacing, Lex Luthor looking guy. He hovered over me and my table for a while with an - 'I'm going to kill you if you cross me' smirk on his face.

There was something evil and sinister in his stare that made me think he might have been a lawyer. As it turned out he is a C. P. A. here in town, he was also Super Jock in High School, oh joy. I had my fill of those people when I was in High School. He and the guy who hired me for that party run in all the local marathons every year in Gaylord. I think Jocko the C. P. A. elected himself spokesman for the others regarding the playing of requests. I have seen him a few times in town over the years and I often wonder if he remembers seeing me during his intoxicated evening at the resort. I seriously doubt that anyone in that class of no class idiots remembers me being in the room with them that night, let alone playing music.

Another break in the action came when a bunch of the delinquents wanted to 'get the band back together' so to speak. Apparently when they were back in school, Wally and Lumpy and Eddie Haskell performed the AC/DC song *Highway to Hell* at the school talent show. At least they wanted to but the school would not let them. Ever since that day the boys in the band adopted *Highway to Hell* as their unofficial class song. They never had the chance to perform it, with air guitar, air bass and air drums, and air groupies I suppose. Oh joy! I suppose they picked *Highway to Hell* as their song, figuring a few of them would end up there some day, hard telling.

The guys set up chairs, grabbed whatever they could find to use as an instrument, a broom, a knife, a breadstick. One guy wrapped a cloth napkin around his head for a headband. They all had cigarettes hanging out of their mouths and wore dark glasses. I am sure this was a laugh riot when they were 17 or 18 years old but that night I wanted to jump up and shout 'You guys are almost 40 years old, grow up!'

They lip-synched the song and played air guitar, air drums and air head. The groupies screamed and writhed around on the floor as if they were in the front row watching the Beatles perform on the *Ed Sullivan Show* in 1964

At the end of this symphony for morons in G - Minor, the boys in the band took their bows as if they had performed at Carnegie Hall. While they were being showered with praise from their loving minions I couldn't help but notice that some of them looked winded. Aside from bending their elbow and shooting the breeze that night, their lip synch act was the most exercise many of them had had since high school.

Toward the end of the night I got a request to play *Paradise by the dashboard light* from Meatloaf. The song is a mini rock opera that really rocks. It is a pretty awesome song and the class of '82 was going to act it out in its entirety.

They formed two lines, guys on one side facing the line of girls on the other like an old fashioned barn dance. The guys sang the Meatloaf part, the girls sang the Ellen Foley part. It was a rowdy rendition of an already boisterous and raunchy song.

My lights were flashing in time to the music and I finally had the place rocking and rolling and everyone seemed to having a good time. Shortly before eleven o'clock, in walked a security guard, a gumshoe, a flat foot, a private dick for hire in an uncomfortable suit. He informed me that the resort manager requested that I shut the party down at eleven.

I announced last call and played the last song. My crowd was not happy but I figured they would get over it. Many of them would not even remember talking to me but that was okay too. It was nice to see them having fun but by eleven I was ready to get out of there and away from these liquored up lunatics.

My car was parked in the circular driveway in front of the resort all night. As I was carrying my DJ equipment to the car I noticed that down the driveway and off to my left, someone was lying on his back on the sidewalk, his legs sticking out into the driveway. He was dead drunk and passed out cold. I just let him lay there. If someone ran over his legs he'd wake up half the man he used to be.

What a night!

6

My achy breaky parts – or –
It's the spinal countdown

In September 1998 I injured my back. I had a pinched-nerve and was barely able to walk or stand for any length of time. When I did walk the pinched-nerve cut off circulation to my feet, which in turn would get fuzzy and numb. One day, I was limping slowly around the Grand Traverse Mall in Traverse City Michigan. I was dependent on a tall walking stick to help me stand up and move around. I stepped off the curb by the main doors of the mall when I got fuzzy feet which gave out and I tumbled onto the ground in front of an oncoming car. Two good Samaritans picked me up and got me back on my feet again. It was embarrassing but given the alternative of being squashed by a Buick, a little embarrassment I could live with. And I am eternally grateful to those Samaritans, whoever and wherever they are.

I had two DJ jobs one right after the other on two consecutive Saturday's that September. As it turned out, those were to be the two worst parties that I have ever played. They were also to be the last parties I was ever going to play.....for quite a long time.

I'm getting a bad reception

The Jordan Valley – Antrim County Michigan

The first of the worst happened in the back yard of a home near East Jordan Michigan. The house was out in the country. It was so hard to find that I wondered if I was in the same country I was when I left the house. A global positioning device would have come in handy that day. Let's face it, Lewis and Clark, a homing pigeon and a star in the east would have come in handy that day.

My back was still pretty bad and I should have canceled that party and the one that followed it. I did not want to let my customers down or leave them stuck without entertainment. I was probably foolish but I had an obligation. As it turned out I should have stayed home.

My pinched-nerve was acting up and my feet were as fuzzy as a college student's head on a Friday night. I strapped my DJ equipment onto a handcart and had to walk across the customer's big back yard to get to the table that was set up for me. This was a farm and the table was set up next to the farmhouse. The back yard was rutted out which I thought must have been caused by gophers. It looked like the grass had only recently grown back in to cover the holes in the ground and you couldn't see them very well. I had a hard enough time walking but this made it worse.

My handcart, which wasn't very sturdy to begin with, wobbled back and forth with every rut and hole that I passed over in the yard. I was about a third of the way to the table when I heard a resounding crash as all my equipment broke loose from the handcart and hit the ground. Needless to say, I was not a happy camper when that happened.

I picked up my things as slowly and painfully as I could and trudged on. The bride was in her 50's or older and had been married before. This was either her second or third or 40th time down the aisle.

I did not have the song the bride wanted for her first dance with the groom, I had to borrow it from her. My back hurt me so much that I did not have my head in the game. I just played any old song I could think of or find. It got so bad that the bride's daughter went through every disc I have to find songs for me to play. She turned the pages in the CD carrying cases, pointing out each song she wanted as if she was pointing out farm animals to a four year old in a children's book. I don't recall having many people on the floor at all that night.

A makeshift wooden dance floor was set up near my table and the house, outside on the lawn. A tent was set up with tables and chairs off to one side. Had I been feeling better things would have gone much smoother. My heart was not in it and I did a really lousy job as a DJ for those people. No one liked a single thing I played and I didn't care so much for my audience either. I just wanted to pack up and go home. If indeed I could even find my way home from that farm house in the wilderness of Antrim County Michigan.

Later in the evening the party was over. A few days went by and I got word that the bride accused me of taking one of her CD's. Her daughter let me borrow it and neither of them could find it. I wrote her a certified letter stating that I placed it on a ledge near the front door of the house. I had enough problems that day, I did not need to compound them by being a thief.

Fiasco on the Hudson – or – See ya later at the nadir

Hudson Twp. Hall – Charlevoix County Michigan

Hudson Township Hall sits about a quarter mile west of the two lane black top known as Camp Ten Road, which runs north out of Otsego County into Charlevoix County between Gaylord and Boyne Falls. That hall is home to a local fire department and its trucks and equipment. The fire department takes up a quarter of the building, the remainder of the building is the banquet hall.

I had played Hudson just a short time before. That reception goes down as one of my shortest wedding receptions ever. It was an alcohol free wedding so the guests gifted and toasted the newlyweds, wolfed down the free vittles and headed for the hills, which was really a shame. With the speed at which the crowd was leaving, you would have thought a nine o'clock curfew for adults had gone into effect that night. I should only have had such luck with the next soiree I played in that very same hall.

I'm getting a bad reception

I arrived at the hall, mid to late afternoon on a warm day in mid September. The hall had a service door at one end of the building that made it easy for me to unload my equipment. I was set up at a table on the east end of the hall. Before me lay a wide open wooden dance floor big enough to land a plane on. At the opposite end of the vast expanses of the dance floor was the head table. The chairs were turned away from me so that the bride and groom and their cronies had their backs to me most of the night. The head table looked out onto a sea of decorated tables squeezed together so as to use every available square inch of walking and breathing room on that side of the building.

Shortly after I arrived, so did the keg. For some reason it was set up along side the dance floor instead of over by the bar counter, conveniently located six miles away on the other side of the gridlock of tables. Two young men who looked to be nowhere near 21, had set up and tapped the keg and were chugging down the suds. I had a really bad feeling about the party. The two bar flies and I were the only people in the hall and the two of them were pickling their livers long before the party had even begun.

Fast forward to a few hours later.

My back was killing me and the hall was warm so I put on a disc and let it play while I stepped outside to get some fresh air. I walked across the dance floor and through the maze of tables and out the east door of the hall. I walked across the front of the building and back to the loading door that I initially used to get into the hall.

There was a group of about twenty, twenty something's standing outside the door smoking and drinking. A few of them looked suspiciously under 21 to me. I approached them but it was dark enough by then that they did not see me. I peered passed them and saw through the open door, into the hall.

Through the door I saw, sitting at my DJ table, a bratty little kid about ten years old monkeying around with my equipment. One of the partiers made a comment about the kid at the table, to which someone else standing nearby replied 'Well he's certainly better than that other guy.' The other guy was yours truly.

Just then, I made my presence known and that shut them up for a microsecond. And then my pinched-nerve acted up again and my feet got fuzzy and numb and gave out on me and I fell on a young woman who screamed as if I had molested her.

There were shrieks of laughter from the bystanders and many snide remarks and I tried to explain that I had a back injury. From somewhere in the crowd I heard someone yell 'Cut him off!' Which was all fine and dandy but I was stone cold sober at the time. Even if I had the slightest interest in throwing a couple back that night, it was twenty miles to my house and I am not willing to destroy my CDL License (required for my bus driving job) for any party.

I got back to my DJ table and shooed little Damien away from my equipment. He might have had the number 666 on his forehead but I did not get close enough to find out. The reception was now a runaway train heading for a brick wall. I played whatever I thought those cretins would like. The people asking for requests got drunker and nastier with every minute. And then I discovered that the groom apparently did not like my sound system so he sent a few of his buddies home to get his.

He must have lived close by because before I knew it this enormous music system with huge tall wooden speakers like giant redwoods compared to mine were brought in.

The bride suddenly decided that after many hours it was time to do the bouquet and garter toss. At that moment I didn't give two hoots in hell what she wanted to toss, unless it was the rest of my deposit money because I was leaving. I did not have to stay there and take that kind of crap from those pea brains. I tracked down the mother of the bride and told her what was what, made sure I got paid, packed up and left around nine-thirty. I was tempted to call the sheriff's department to report some potentially intoxicated drivers in the vicinity of the hall, but I refrained.

The next day, the mother of the bride called me to see if I was okay. Personally I think she was hoping to hear that I was not mad or planning on suing. I told her I was fine (lying) and I asked her how the rest of the party went.

'Oh it was just wonderful. The boys played their music all night and everybody danced and laughed and had a great time.' She bubbled on and on as if trying to sell the uninitiated, a trip to Disney World.

I did not believe her for a minute but at least she paid me. A few days after the party, I attended a meeting after work. I am a county bus driver and my feet gave out again and I crash-landed on the concrete floor in the garage at work. I saw a doctor the next day and was off work from September 1998 – January 1999.

I did not play again for a year.

And after a long stretch of time had passed, I was debating whether to go back to playing music at partys or giving it up completely.

Eventually I decided that I wanted to continue as an occasional DJ so I searched around online for new equipment. It cost a pretty penny but I bought a professional quality DJ dual CD player with a sound mixer board with an amplifier. This gave me the ability to switch seamlessly from song to song with no breaks in the music. I no longer had to lug around an extra speaker just to talk on a microphone since I could just plug the microphone directly into the mixer itself. I bought a pair of EV© brand speakers that seem to weigh a ton each and are mighty powerful at 175 watts apiece. The only remaining piece of original equipment I had was the trusty old Magnavox receiver, which the speakers connected to. I also purchased a set of four stage lights with multi colored gels on them that move to the beat of the music.

Over the years I have added new toys to my repertoire such as a cordless microphone system which has come in handy on many occasions such as toasts, announcements and the like. These events are made all the more enjoyable without having to drag around or trip over a long tangled up electrical cord. I am a novice technology geek and I think this stuff is pretty cool.

In the fall, many years ago I was down in Lansing Michigan just a week or two prior to Halloween. I went to the Meridian Mall in nearby Okemos, which had a Spencer's Gifts. The store was having a sale on all of their Halloween lighting. I picked up a red and blue rotating police light as well as a rotating, multi colored disco ball and a bubble machine.

I'm getting a bad reception

I live about 170 miles from that particular store and I wanted to see if my new toys worked before I took them home. My hotel was the Radisson in downtown Lansing and I lugged everything up to the room and set it all up like a little kid unpacking his bounty on Christmas morning. One by one I turned everything on and filled the bubble machine. I shut off all the lights in the room and as the hippies might say the room looked 'trippy, wow man, for sure, really.'

My room was on the fifth floor and the window looked west out onto downtown Lansing and the Capital building. It was dark outside by the time I got everything set up and I can only imagine what people on the street were thinking if they happened by chance to look up and see the Willie Wonka style, psychadelic bubble and light show going on up in my room.

For sure, really.

In the summer of 2006 I bought a pair of Chauvet © brand multi colored light bars, each being the size of a toolbox. These new light bars are worlds brighter and more powerful that the previous lights I had as well as being much more compact and easier to tote around. The lights are also much brighter than most of the people I play for but that's a whole other matter entirely. These new lights pulse to the beat of the music and really light up the hall.

I gave up on cassettes simply because CD's are so much easier to use. Over the years I have amassed over 700 CD's. I find sometimes that it is hard to keep up with current trends in music because they change with the frequency of a traffic signal.

I focus primarily on weddings now and pick one up every so often. What a long strange trip down the aisle it has been. Every component of every wedding I have ever played has had enough adventure to merit its own chapter in this book. What follows is a compilation of those adventures that I have titled:

Anatomy of a wedding

7

The Wedding Rehearsal – or –
Antici-pay-ay-shun is making me wait

Irontone Springs Roadside Park – Gaylord, Michigan

Until a few years ago I had only played the music for the reception and that was that. In the summer of 2005, a new chapter of my DJ history began, when I started playing the music for the ceremony itself. The wedding was for the son of one of my fellow employees and it took place at Irontone Springs Roadside Park on Old U.S. 27, just a few miles north of Gaylord.

Years before I – 75 sliced Otsego County in half on its way from Crawford County (south), to Cheboygan County (north); U. S. 27 was the only road available to take motorists to The Upper Peninsula. Travelers whose final destination was St. Ignace or Sault Saint Marie or points west, had to wait upwards of fourteen hours for car ferries to transport them across the treacherous Straits of Mackinaw.

Interstate 75 winds and meanders its way from Miami Florida to its final destination at the International Bridge in Sault Saint Marie.

I'm getting a bad reception

On November 1, 1957, the Mackinaw Bridge, which proudly sits across the Straits, was opened to accommodate the swarms of motorists who previously lost many hours of theirs lives in line waiting for the car ferries to arrive.

Back in those pre-Interstate days, you had to drive on U.S. 27 in order to get to Mackinaw, or take your chances on dirt roads to get there faster. As you drove out of Gaylord, you passed right by the aforementioned Irontone Springs Roadside Park. The park is lush with trees and plant life, more than likely fed by the natural spring and the babbling brook that runs through the center of it. The park has a picnic shelter, outdoor grills as well as picnic tables. The main feature of the park is the large wooden footbridge, which hangs over the brook. In its heyday the park was quite a nice little tourist attraction as well as a resting place for weary travelers heading north to Mackinaw.

The park is conveniently located just around the bend on U.S. 27 from Livingston Township Hall. As you will read, many of the weddings I have played at Irontone Springs, end up at the hall. Better to have the guests gathered in one space than to have them wandering around Otsego County like lost sheep.

Lately the park and the hall have become quite a hot spot for weddings, like the first of which I played there in that summer of 2005. The footbridge makes an ideal place for pictures as well as a place for the bridal party and the bride and groom to cross symbolically into married life.

Normally the task of performing wedding ceremony music is taken care of in a church by an organist sequestered somewhere in a corner. There is no way to get an organist and his or her instrument out to a park unless you uproot them, put them on a flatbed truck and haul them out there. These days there are many portable keyboards that can simulate every sound in the orchestra. I have no musical talent and cannot even so much as play *Chopsticks*. I cannot even EAT with chopsticks, let alone play the tune of the same name on the keyboard.

I like the element of surprise that comes with appearing at a hall with a carload of equipment and giving the audience a great night of dance music. I usually have a great deal of contact with my brides over the phone but never see them until the big day. The bride is always easy to spot. She is the one in the white dress with the stress on face.

When I was asked to play at that wedding ceremony, I was not crazy about the idea. I had to meet a group of complete strangers who were caught up in the last minute stress of a wedding. It also meant I had to show up to play for the rehearsal as well, to give the bride and groom and associates, some idea of when to enter, where to stand, etc. Much like the final rehearsals for a play, there is a great deal of confusion at a wedding rehearsal and who needs a stranger with a boom box whom nobody knows. I was nervous enough playing for the reception, meeting the whole crowd at the reception, especially under such tense conditions, was too much pressure. Lately however I have come to appreciate my pre-wedding introduction to those I will eventually be playing for the following day. It is a nice way to break the ice and meeting them eases some of my nervousness as well.

Thankfully I knew the mother of the groom at that first wedding at Irontone Springs so I was not completely anonymous. I was introduced to her son as well as the bride and various assorted relatives and friends. There was not much for me to do until the rehearsal started so I just stood back and watched the chaos.

What I observed at the first rehearsal has been replayed at every other rehearsal and ceremony that I have been involved with only with different people.

The Bride either looks excited or scared to death or any combination of both. She is the center of attention and the eye of the storm. When not being bombarded by a thousand questions, she can usually be spotted standing off to one side laughing with her bridesmaids.

The Groom is usually standing off to another side goofing around with his friends, laughing and joking to cover up his nervousness and not taking much of the madness seriously. More than likely his mind is on the party after the rehearsal, how much alcohol he is going to consume at the reception or his chances at getting lucky on the wedding night.

The Mothers in the crowd are as busy as bees and have the diplomacy of contract negotiators. I've seen them send so and so back to the house or the hotel or the car because so and so forgot something. The Mothers, who are just as nervous and emotional as the bride, dole out orders with amazing efficiency. They can always cry later after the ceremony but for now, at the rehearsal, they are in charge of the million and one little details and chores that have to be done before the service.

The Fathers, at least the ones that I have seen, look like sideline observers watching a traffic accident. They sense that what they are witnessing is beyond them and they cannot do much except get out of the way. They usually joke around with the other men and discuss fishing or football or anything but the wedding and their emotions.

Someone will inevitably be late, some out of town guest will not have shown up yet or acknowledge if they were attending the wedding at all. Well we can't start without him (or her), a few times the delay has been because the minister or the Justice of the Peace is late for the rehearsal. The celebrant, nine time out of ten arrives, sees the crowd and has this 'What have I gotten myself into this time' look on his face. Yet he valiantly puts on a brave front and tries to get down to the business at hand.

Most of the brides I have played for at Irontone have made good use of the picturesque footbridge over the babbling brook. I think many brides are frustrated stage directors who have in mind exactly how their special day should be choreographed. At Irontone Springs, the bride and groom and bridal party huddle in the parking lot on the other side of the footbridge, and finally, here is where I come in. Once the players are in place, the celebrant and the groom will enter. When they are in place, I begin playing a song for the entry of the bridal party, when they are in place, I switch gears to a different song for the bride and her father. There is more on the specific songs for each of these phases of the service in the next chapter.

Most likely, someone will not be able to hear any of the music for any part of the service and yell for me to 'TURN IT UP, WE CAN'T HEAR IT!' And I happily oblige. When someone yells that at the rehearsal, I pray they get it out of their system and don't shout it out at the ceremony.

Getting the bride and groom and their wedding party in their places takes up more time than the actual ceremony itself. Once everybody is at the 'altar', the celebrant says 'I'm going to say "Blah blah blah – then when I am done – more blah blah blah, do you so and so take so and so for their lawfully wedded so and so, "'they exchange the rings and so on and so on. The Bride and Groom practice their vows, the Mothers are crying, the Fathers look bored, the Groomsmen are fidgeting, the Bridesmaids are giggly and somewhere, three or four kids are running around unsupervised. And yours truly, once the celebrant pretends to declare the happy couple to be 'man and wife' (Applause Applause Applause) – I hit the music and the newlyweds walk back down the aisle.

And then we do it a few more times.

* * * * *

There was a wedding that took place at Irontone Springs a few years later where the bride and groom had not returned any of my papers and did not let me know what songs they wanted until I brought it to their attention at the rehearsal. Now this was at the rehearsal for their wedding that was then less than 24 hours away and they had no clue as to what they wanted for their first dance, the bridal party dance, or any of the specialty dances. This would not have been such a big deal but I had been in close contact with that particular bride for months leading to her wedding.

The bride went around asking people what they thought would be good songs for the special songs at her wedding. I guess the thought of special music never crossed her mind. I am not sure if a deep thought ever made that same journey either. It is pretty bad when the bride has her DJ pick out her songs but thankfully I have played enough weddings to know what songs are appropriate for all occasions. Boy oh boy, talk about being flying by the seat of my pants. Had I not brought the songs to her attention, she might not have had a second thought about it. She barely had a FIRST thought about it.

The bride chose a song called *I loved her first* by a group called Heartland, for the Father / Daughter dance. I had never heard of either that song or that group and it was getting too late to run to Wal-Mart to look for the song. After I left the park, I went home and found that song on I – Tunes. And I let out a big sigh or relief later that night as I was loading the song onto the disc so I could play it at the reception.

I'm getting a bad reception

Treetops North Golf Resort – Gaylord Michigan

Wedding rehearsal ala cart

There was the wedding, which took place on the 18th green of Treetops North Golf Resort, where Lee Trevino and Phil Mickelson have played in a par three shootout. I'm not much into golf that doesn't have a windmill or an alligator or a putt putt, but Treetops North Resort is beautiful and impressive.

The 18th green had a million dollar view of the valley below. I think it most likely cost that much to play golf there, let alone holding a wedding ceremony, just a hunch.

To get to the green you had to cross the paved golf cart path that led to the clubhouse and the cart return. During the rehearsal it was all you could do to dodge the incoming carts that were going fast enough to qualify for NASCAR. They were supposed to temporarily close the ramp for the ceremony but I imagined the following scenario:

> Preacher: Do you take this woman….
> Golf cart: VROOOOOOOOOOOOM!
> Preacher: ….to be your lawfully wedded….
> Golf cart: SCREEEEEEEEEEEEEEEECH!
> Preacher: I know pronounce you, a hole in one.

The carts were whizzing by and the rehearsal took place on the 18th green. For the wedding there was going to be about a hundred chairs set up with an aisle down the center. There was going to be a podium with a microphone plugged in to a nearby speaker on a stand. Off to one side would be a wooden table set up for my trusty boom box.

I arrived for the rehearsal carrying my trusty boom box in hand and a puzzled look on my face. I was not exactly sure if I was in the right place so I went into the clubhouse to see if I was where I was supposed to be. The young man at the desk called around and found out that the wedding party was in the resort's shuttle van on the way up to the clubhouse.

I'm getting a bad reception

Treetops North sits about three miles north of Treetops Resort. The wedding party and assorted guests were in the shuttle bus on the way up to wedding site when I called to find out their location. I was happy to be in the right place. The clubhouse sits about two miles down at the end of a long, scenic driveway running through rich green fairways and rich expensive condos.

The bride, who was known as 'The Princess' all through her youth, arrived wearing a light summer dress and a tiara and a veil on her head. She also looked terrified.

There was the usual chatter and goofing around. I had the routine down pat by then and I waited until I was needed to play the songs for the rehearsal. We ran through the service a few times and I went home to relax a little before the big day.

During the weekend of that wedding, Northern Michigan was experiencing an unbearable heat wave. The heat and humidity, which would have been normal for Palm Springs in July, was horrible for Northern Michigan in June.

I wore shorts and a nice shirt for the rehearsal and the bride requested that I wear a three-piece suit for the actual service. The last time I put on a suit was 1989 when I was in a play. I am a jeans and polo shirt and maybe a sweater when it gets cool kind of guy. Nothing fancy for me except for church casual for services on Sunday, that's it. I was not crazy about being in a suit so being in one on a real scorcher of a day was even worse.

The one thing that made that weekend tolerable was the fact that it was windy. I am not sure what my internal temperature was that day while I was up there baking on the hill with the others but I am pretty sure that if I was a meat loaf I would have been done in an hour.

8

The ceremony:
I got the Muzak in me – or –
I now denounce you man and wife

I like to set the mood with music early on. When people gather for a wedding there should be a sense of excitement and a little pageantry in the air. There should be love and joy among the congregation on the occasion of two people becoming one. Most people have the above sentiments but some also have the love of free beer and the joy of free food, but that is another story.

I figure if I am asked to play for the bride to make her grand entrance, as well as the bride and groom's first steps together, I might as well play for everything. Not every song in my catalog mind you, but for the entire service, such as it is.

When I am asked to play for the ceremony I arrive early at the location with my trusty boom box in hand and a few CD's at the ready. As people filter in I crank up the Kenny G. Well, as much as you can actually crank up Kenny G. without feeling like you are in a dentist office or an elevator.

I'm getting a bad reception

The mellow sounds of Kenny G. waft over the gathering crowd as they take their seats. I have played a few weddings where they didn't even have seats. The crowd just stood there mixing and mingling under the picnic shelter or by the barbecue or the swing set.

At the appropriate time the groom and the preacher (or Justice of the Peace) enter the scene and walk together down the aisle. Next, it is time for the bridesmaid and ushers to make their entrance.

Gradually it comes time to snuff out Kenny G. By 'snuff out' I don't mean in the way Tony Soprano would snuff somebody out. I mean by the flip of a switch and changing the music to a beautiful instrumental piece called *The Trumpet Voluntary.*

Many moons ago when I was in the school choir, there was an upperclassman that played *The Trumpet Voluntary* each year at the Christmas concert. The tune is very regal and it makes you feel like you are sitting at Buckingham Palace instead of sitting on metal folding chairs (or standing by the barbecue or the swing set) in the park. I think the song was played during the wedding of Prince Charles and Lady Di in the summer of 1981. When Charles married Camilla Parker Bowles, the orchestra could have easily played the theme from Mr. Ed. After all 'a horse is a horse of course of course.'

'Trumpet Voluntary' – Bridal Party entrance music

Trumpet Voluntary is the title of several English keyboard pieces from the Baroque era. Most commonly played on the organ (they are utilizing the trumpet stop, hence the name), they generally consist of a slow introduction followed by a flamboyant faster section with the right hand playing fanfare-like figures over a simple accompaniment in the left hand.

The organist and composer John Stanley wrote a number of trumpet voluntaries, as did many of his lesser contemporaries. The most famous piece known by that name, however, is a composition by Jeremiah Clarke, properly a rondo for keyboard named Prince of Denmark's March. This piece was incorrectly attributed to Henry Purcell for many years, particularly in a well-known arrangement for trumpet, string orchestra and organ by Sir Henry Wood.

-----From wikipedia.com

I'm getting a bad reception

Once the bridal party has gathered by the altar (or the barbecue or the swing set), I switch over to *Here comes the bride*. I once had someone at a wedding ask me if I ever play the wedding ceremony songs in their entirety. I don't usually because a few of the songs go on for a good five or six minutes. The bride and groom just want to do the 'I do' do-se-do and get out of there. So I cut the music when necessary. The bride is escorted by her father who by custom has an, 'I'm losing my baby and this wedding is costing me a fortune' look on his face.

'Here comes the bride'

The "Bridal Chorus" from the opera Lohengrin, by German composer Richard Wagner, is the standard march played for the bride's entrance at most formal weddings in the United States and at many weddings throughout the Western world. In English-speaking countries it is generally known as "Here Comes the Bride" or "Wedding March" (though actually "wedding march" refers to any song accompanying the entrance or exit of the bride, most often Felix Mendelssohn's "Wedding March"). However, it is seldom played at Jewish weddings, due to Wagner's reputation as an anti-semite and the Nazis' use of his music. It is also not used by the Lutheran Church - Missouri Synod because of various factors, but most especially due to the perceived pagan connotations of Wagner's plays. The Roman Catholic Church generally does not allow the Bridal Chorus at Catholic weddings due to the fact that it is a secular piece of music.

Its usual placement at the beginning of a wedding ceremony is not entirely in accordance with its placement in the opera. In the opera, the chorus is sung after the ceremony by the women of the wedding party, as they accompany the heroine Elsa to the bridal chamber. In addition, the marriage between Elsa and Lohengrin is an almost immediate failure.

-----From wikipedia.com

The music fades out when the bride and her escort arrive and the preacher or the Justice of the Peace start the ceremony.

I'm getting a bad reception

Most of the outdoor wedding ceremonies I have played have been relatively short. I have been to a few Catholic weddings as a guest where it was advisable to pack a lunch and a change of clothes because you were going to be there a while.

Backyard wedding on Otsego Lake, Gaylord Michigan

Smart Alec

The wedding took place in a back yard of a home on Otsego Lake, five miles south of Gaylord Michigan. Outside of some news footage of the Sturgis Run in South Dakota, I have never seen so many piercings and tattoos on one group of people in one place as I did at that wedding. They turned out to be one of the best groups I have ever played for.

The bride's sister came over to me and asked 'Excuse me, but has anyone ever told you that you look like somebody famous?'

Gentle reader it will help you to know that I am a white male when I tell you I replied: 'Yes, all the time.......Oprah!'

The young lady insisted I looked like Alec Baldwin. Frankly I don't see it. I used to weigh 318 pounds and thought I looked like either John Goodman or Roseanne Barr or both. I happen to like both John Goodman and Roseanne Barr so that was just a comparison, not an insult. I am some fifty pounds lighter now and I suppose I could look like somebody famous. I have done enough stupid things in my life to be the back end of Mr. Ed. But when I look in the mirror (after the shock wears off) I don't see Alec Baldwin.

Back to the back yard: There was the usual amount of picture taking. I spotted a stocky bleach blond woman, an aunt I think, who called herself 'The Outcast of the Family'. She was leaning against the back end of my car. Someone came by and wanted to take a picture when Auntie Outcast grabbed me by the arm and pulled me over to her and said 'I want my picture taken next to Mr. Baldwin here.' I was flattered but I think I look more like Fred Flintstone on most days than Mr. Baldwin. Yabba dabba doo.

The party in the back yard took place on a picture perfect blue-sky day in June. The reception was just down the street at yet another golf course/campground/resort called Beaver Creek. The hall was a log building that sat on top of a hill at the highest point on the property. The resort had a waterslide and from the screened in balcony of the hall you could look out and see the campground down in the valley, the valley so low.

The hall was not very big and looked like the rec. room of a big house. There were tables and chairs set up for about 75 to 100 wedding guests. Scattered through the room were comfortable log sofas and chairs and tables. The room reminded me of the Lincoln Logs I had when I was a kid.

There was an enclosed porch, which served as the smoking section. There was a full service kitchen and off in a corner of the main room was a big screen TV. Most of the male guests drifted over to the set and watched NASCAR at one time or another that night. They had a lot of time to watch TV. This was a day where the wedding started at two, lasted five minutes and dinner, if you were lucky, began some time before midnight. Dinner actually got served around six-thirty, but it might as well have been midnight for as long as it took.

I should also mention that the hall on the hill was hell to get to. From the parking lot there were twelve cement steps leading up to a sidewalk. From the sidewalk to the hall was a creaky wooden ramp like the kind you would use to get on a ride at Disney World. I expected to see a sign hanging overhead saying 'You are now one hour away from attending this wedding reception.'

I had my DJ equipment strapped to my four-wheeled push cart and it weebled and wobbled all the way up the creaky wooden gangplank. If I had known about the climb I would have hired a mountain Sherpa or the Von Trapp children to help me climb every mountain.

Irontone Springs roadside park: The Sequel

I played a ceremony on a very humid and cloudy day. The air was thick and unstable, much like Rosie O'Donnell, and a stray and angry looking cloud drifted by. The cloud rolled in and got scarier looking by the minute. There was an occasional snap of thunder but nothing serious, until the wedding started.

The wedding was just about to start and the bridal party was all lined up when suddenly there was a loud explosion of thunder; which

70

sounded as if someone fired a cannon down the street and blew up the hall. The assembly that was mixing and mingling and lingering, suddenly scattered like cockroaches when you turn on the light in the kitchen in the middle of the night. Most of the crowd went over to the metal roofed picnic shelter. In the panic of the moment it did not occur to anyone that they were standing under a potential lightning rod that was the metal picnic shelter in the middle of an approaching storm. It was a miracle they were not all zapped into oblivion right then and there or turned into a big pile of French fries in formal wear.

The clouds were just noisy and boisterous but no rain had fallen. I started the music for the bridal party and finally the bride. And eventually the preacher announced the couple as man and wife. They kissed, they turned and they moved down the aisle as if they were the next contestants on *The Price is Right*. When they took their first steps into married life, I played the traditional Recessional.

Mendelssohn's Wedding March – Bride and Groom recessional

Mendelssohn's "Wedding March" is one of the best known of the pieces that he wrote as incidental music for A Midsummer Night's Dream in 1842. It is one of the most played wedding marches in the world.

At weddings in many English-speaking countries, this piece is commonly used as a recessional, though frequently stripped of its episodes in this context.

The first time it was used at a wedding was when Dorothy Carew wed Tom Daniel at St Peter's Church, Tiverton, UK, on 2 June 1847. However it did not become popular at weddings until it was selected by Victoria, The Princess Royal for her marriage to the Crown Prince of Prussia on January 25, 1858.

An organ on which Mendelssohn gave recitals of amongst others the "Wedding March" is housed in St Ann's Church in Tottenham.

------From wikipedia.com

The songs for the ceremony were strictly a guess as to what would be appropriate for the occasion. When the bridal party arrives I could have played *Hail hail the gang's all* here but I chose *Trumpet Voluntary.* When the bride arrives I could have played *Hail to the Chief* but I chose *Here comes the bride.* And instead of the Recessional I could have played *Ease on down the road* from *The Wiz.*

It took some doing to find the songs that came to be my wedding ceremony standards. When I first did the ceremonies, the songs were spread out over three different discs. I put them all together on one disc, which made it much easier to switch from track to track at the appropriate time.

The bride and groom and their bridal party stand to one side and form a receiving line. My work is done, at least for the ceremony and I slink off to one side and head to the hall.

From there, it is all over but the shouting, and the eating and the dancing, sometimes all at the same time.

9

Dinner:
I get too hungry, for dinner at eight – or –
Whiskey for my men, beer for my horses, and
Ritalin for the children

Dinner at weddings has its pros and cons for me. On the pro side, I get a great meal. I've had everything from prime rib to Polish sausage as well as chickens of all denominations and preparations. I make sure to eat a good meal at every wedding reception because I have a long night ahead of me. A hungry DJ is not a happy DJ. And an unhappy, hungry DJ is capable of eating the furniture by the end of the night. And there's not much meat on a folding chair unless of course someone is sitting on it.

In the DJ information packet which I send to every customer, there is a questionnaire in which I ask 'What time do you want me to start playing dance music?' 'What time do you want me to stop?' Approximately. For every 'approximately', there is that gray area known as dinner music. This is the void between the wedding ceremony and dancing parts of the evening. Under   normal circumstances I throw on a little 'lite jazz' or soft rock while people are mixing and mingling and noshing.

Dinner music is not my favorite part of the evening. It seems to drag on endlessly and I would much prefer just to get the music and the audience cranked up and dancing. Dinner music is a necessary evil at a wedding. The family and friends and relatives and strangers need time to unwind and get to know one another before they eat dinner and later put a lampshade on their head and pretend they are hysterically funny. After the ceremony, I like to be at the hall, setting up and getting ready. I want to be part of the scenery when the first guest arrives. As mentioned, I am not crazy about the dinner music portion of the night but I would never just arrive at the hall and set up during dinner. That would be distracting and put me under incredible pressure. In the long run it is worth it to have people see me from the get go. Or is that the gecko?

Anyway, my goal is to be at the hall with enough equipment set up so that I can announce the bride and groom and the wedding party and their kith and kin and Jerry Mathers as the Beaver. From the first announcement I construct the rest of my DJ setup while the guests are chattering away and munching their crackers and cheese.

Eventually I will have all of my equipment set up, and since I don't want to stand there with my finger in my tokas not playing anything, I feel obligated to play something, anything. Most of the time, dinner starts soon after the bride and groom arrive. However, there are other times when I don't think we're going to eat before midnight.

After the ceremony, when the guests usually disperse or stay to converse, it is time for pictures. After the wedding photographer and Aunt Gertie with an Instamatic and several cousins twice removed, stalk the newlyweds all over creation, putting them through every possible sitting, standing combination by every tree, rock or waterfall, the party heads my way and everything shifts to the hall.

Bride and Groom arrive at the hall:
Matt: Ladies and gentlemen_____

When I first started as a DJ I used to get to the hall ridiculously early. I wanted to allow plenty of 'just in case I need to run home and get something' time. Whatever minor disasters I may have imagined haven't happened so far. It has gotten so I can set up my DJ equipment within minutes of unloading it from my car, with plenty of time to announce the bride and groom. I bring enough music to last a week, or until the bride and groom's first anniversary.

Normally, as mentioned, I throw on a little light music after I announce the bride and groom. And that is usually no longer than an hour. Sometimes however I play dinner music longer than I do dance music.

Irontone Springs: Redux

Yet another wedding took place at Irontone Springs. It was a picture perfect day. I was even there with my trusty boom box that faithfully belted out *'Here comes the bride'* and the traditional recessional.

The bride and groom were married on a hillside next a barbecue on a metal pole. The Justice of the Peace performed the service in microseconds. The wedding began at two o'clock and ended at two oh three and a half. They had the reception at Livingston Township Hall, just around the corner from the park.

Livingston Hall is really a shoebox with central heating and air conditioning but it has been the hall that I have played the most. The reason being, it is the most reasonably priced hall in Otsego County. You walk in the double doors and to your immediate left is a small meeting room, after that a kitchen, after that restrooms. On the opposite wall is a door to the outside with a dozen or so tables along the far wall. Another wall makes up the north side of the building. There are doors leading to a storage area for table and chairs, further along is an archway leading to a bar and another outside door. The next wall brings you back to the beginning as you pass by a dozen or so tables on that side of the building. In the center of the room is a dance floor.

For reasons unknown the wedding was at two, with dinner scheduled at six. I had my equipment all set up right next to the front door of the hall and it was hard for me to hide. Since I played for the micro ceremony I got to the hall and stood watch over my equipment all afternoon until the reception. The bar wasn't supposed to open until the bride and groom arrived and at the snail's pace of the afternoon, the bride and groom weren't going to arrive until their first child graduated high school.

Naturally, people started arriving at the hall and wanted to party. Or they wanted a nap, and they could have had one for as long as it took to eat. I have over 700 CD's in my collection and I think I played 683 of them between the 'I do's' and the first bite of dinner.

I had one feisty little old crumpet who came over to my DJ table and wanted me to play 'spunky' dancing music because she wanted to party. I told her I play the lighter stuff around dinner and then crank it up later. Well she wanted me to crank it up NOW. Either that or she wanted someone to crank HER up now.

I had several people come up to me in quick succession and insist I get the party music going. Once again, like Maria Von Trapp in *The Sound of Music,* I had to explain that I had to 'start at the very beginning, a very good place to start.' Slower music first, dinner, formal dances then the rowdier stuff. If I had to explain that to one more person I was going to have it printed up on cards and hand them out.

The guests couldn't drink because the bar wasn't open. They couldn't dance because that stubborn DJ wasn't playing fast music. They gathered in packs and started roaming around like hungry wolves on the prairie. I guess they thought I was somehow responsible for more than entertainment because they started getting nasty and impatient with ME.

There were some antsy kids at the party. Several of them came over to me at regular intervals and wanted to hear some dance music. I was bored to tears by then and was looking for something to do so I played the *YMCA* and the *Chicken Dance.*

Meanwhile, it seemed like eight days went by between the ceremony and dinner. I was standing guard over my equipment, fending off people who want to hear something faster than Kenny G. Which would be just about ANYBODY. The caterers were working diligently in the kitchen. To stave off a massive hunger induced riot, they put out bowls of snacks on some tables. The ravenous guests went after them like a crow goes after a dead squirrel on the highway.

The bride and groom finally arrived. It took them so long to get to the hall I was close to forgetting their names. A few minutes longer and I would have forgotten MY name. Whoever I am. And after eons of waiting, the bar finally opened and the reaction was similar to the end of Prohibition.

Getting the bride and groom to the hall was one thing, keeping them there was another issue. It was a beautiful day and there is no smoking allowed in the hall. So every chance he got, such as three seconds after he got there, the groom went outside so smoke with his buddies. I thought for a moment that the bride and groom might actually have been the same person. For a while I never saw them in the same room together at the same time. This was sort of like Elizabeth Montgomery when she played both Samantha and her cousin Serena on *Bewitched.*

Eventually, after many moons had passed, we finally settled down to eat. By then the guests had waited so long I expected them to get up and sing 'Food glorious food' from *Oliver.*

The food had either been cooking too long and was as tired of waiting as the rest of us, or was not on the burner long enough. I had prime rib, which I thought was going to be a treat, instead it was so raw I expected it to still be mooing when I stuck a fork in it.

It took such a long time to eat that a few people left before dinner started. I was even considering throwing on a long CD and leaving myself, and I don't think anyone would have noticed. After dinner, the groom and or bride and a combination of both made several trips outside to light up a smoke.

Finally we got around to the specialty dances. There was the bride and groom's first dance. Exit stage left to go out and puff. There was the bridal party dance. Smoke smoke smoke. There was the father daughter dance. Smoke smoke smoke. Then there was the mother son dance. Smoke smoke smoke. They sent up enough smoke to attract the Cherokee Nation.

Aside from the lethargy and starvation of waiting four hours to eat, there were the glaring differences between the bride and groom's family. The members of the groom's family were ordinary, working class folks, earthy, down home and lots of fun. The members of the bride's side of the family sat on the opposite side of the hall and acted like they were the Duke and Duchess of York, or should that be Dork.

Just when things were getting revved up on the dance floor, the bride and groom did the Dollar Dance. Shortly after the Dollar Dance the bride's side of the family started clearing the tables, folding them up and stacking metal chairs. The groom's side of the family was ready to party but the tables and chairs were vanishing from the room as if being swept up in a tornado.

There was some discrepancy over which family was paying for what. The bride's family folded their tents, as it were, as well as the tables and chairs on their side of the reception hall and left. The reception was over at nine-thirty. I'm surprised the marriage made it to nine forty-five.

Whiskey for my men, beer for my horses:
And Ritalin for the children

I have witnessed some outlandish behavior at wedding receptions. Most of which will be, or has already been, discussed elsewhere in this book. Outlandish behavior usually comes from free flowing spirits and the people who love them. The following is dedicated to another source of outlandish behavior that many people bring with them to weddings, children.

I am not good with kids. I often joke that I didn't like children, even when I WAS, a children. Some people do. Some people are such terrific parents they would make Ward and June Cleaver proud, more power to them. I am the youngest of three, and there were eight and ten years between my brother and sister and myself. I spent a lot of time by myself and was pretty shy for most of my youth. Now that I am youth less, so to speak, I am not kid friendly.

I have walked in to many local meeting halls, Eagles Clubs and the like, that were magically transformed for one night into beautiful show places. You'd never guess that in some of those halls a few days earlier, eight or nine people sat at a long wooden table, on cold metal chairs, discussing zoning laws and dog license fees.

Many halls that I have played were decorated with elaborate lights draped in see through fabric and suspended from the ceiling with a centerpiece hanging over the dance floor. The tables were adorned with centerpieces, odds and ends of décor, confetti and bowls full of snacks such as pretzels or after dinner mints. People generally inhale those mints the minute they see them. I have seen disposable cameras set on every table allowing the guests to capture the magic of the evening. I have also seen streamers and balloons on strings. Those are either tied to tables or weighed down by smaller balloons filled with water. There is as much time and energy involved with decorating a hall for a wedding reception as there is in decorating the stage for a Broadway show.

Kids and balloons go together like Britney Spears and rehab. I have seen on far too many occasions, lovely and expensive party decorations become weapons of mass destruction in the hands of hoards of hyper little ankle biters.

It is amazing that a toddler or tyke can grab a balloon from a table, run up to another kid and hit him or her with it. This sets off a chain reaction where in they'll start chasing each other like the Coyote chasing the Road Runner. Boredom and sugar give children the speed of a NASCAR driver. Their feisty little legs go at warp speed. If adults could move that fast, we'd all weigh 98 pounds.

Meanwhile, back at the brat pack, one kid becomes two kids, then four, then six and their little group can appear to multiply like microbes in a Petri dish. The running and the screaming and the mayhem that ensues, often makes me want to step outside for a few moments of peace and quiet and sedatives.

Oh and did I mention the screaming?

I have heard little girls at wedding receptions scream such high notes that only dogs and low flying aircraft can hear them.

I can only imagine that adults bring their little kids to wedding receptions because it is a cheap babysitter. All you have to do is walk into the hall, unleash the hellions on a room full of unsuspecting strangers while you wolf down free food and drink, then pick up your little sprout some time after last call. By then, most of the guests are orbiting the Earth in an alcohol-fueled stupor and the once beautifully decorated hall looks like London after the Blitz.

This of course does not apply to every parent or child at every reception, just the noisier and more memorable ones.

I have seen otherwise responsible parents suddenly become Helen Keller. They let the little monsters loose and suddenly do not see, hear or have the ability to communicate with their kids. At one recent party, the buffet tables were set up on the dance floor before dinner and the kids discovered that the floor length table cloths made the area underneath the tables a great place to play.

I'm getting a bad reception

It is a shame that well-intentioned parents dress their kids to the nines for weddings, knowing how antsy they get. Recently I saw a little girl at a reception dressed in what looked to be a kid sized wedding gown with everything but the veil. She screamed like a police siren. Her shoes vanished and when she wasn't running through the hall at the speed of light, she was writhing around on the floor like Madonna at the MTV Video Music Awards.

Little boys don't fare much better. I've seen too many little guys, usually in the wedding party, dressed up in a tux, the whole nine yards. By the end of the night they have the shoes off, their hair is ruffled, the jacket and tie are missing in action. One half of their button down shirt is either unbuttoned or un-tucked and they look like they've just come off a three-day bender.

It is the parents right to being their little darlings to a wedding and the reception, to each their own. Perhaps children at a wedding reception, especially those who are overly rambunctious and uncontrolled can serve as a first strike method of birth control. Listening to a tribe of screaming banshees for six or seven hours could make a newlywed couple reconsider creating their own little dumplings later that night when the reception is over.

Works for me.

10

The bride and groom's first dance - or –
Dr. Jekyll and Mrs. Bride

The custom of a "First Dance" harkens back to ancient times when the "Bride Kidnapper" would show off his "hunting" skills by parading his "stolen" bride around, in front of his warrior friends, so they could see how well he had done. The feasting would begin immediately after this display. Today, the "First Dance" still traditonally marks the beginning of the reception.
-----From 'www.hudsonvalleyweddings.com

It is amazing to me that at nearly five dollars a pack, people are still coughing up (pun intended) the money to put a flaming stick of expensive dried leaves in their mouths. To each his or her own I guess but smoking never interested me. I grew up in a house full of smokers and seeing those huge ashtrays teeming with butts, as well as the smell, was a turnoff.

You cannot smoke in most of the halls that I have played. This makes it great for me, but I am the entertainment, not the star of the day. The bride and groom and the bridal party, if they smoke, spend most of their time just outside the door of the hall. On a sunny summer day when the sun goes down at ten o'clock, I may play for hours and not see a dancer on the floor. Sometimes the floor is so empty you would have thought they evacuated the hall and did not bother to tell me about it. On rainy days, I have a more attentive crowd because no matter how much you want to light one up, you don't want to spend the night in wet clothing.

Once all traces of dinner have been cleared away, it is time to move to the next phase of the wedding reception, the bride and groom's first dance. I usually let the bride and or groom make the call on when they want to do this. They are having such a good time socializing and smoking and chugging free drinks that they seem to forget this gateway dance that leads to the faster portion of the evening. If the bride and groom are hanging around outside with their friends, it is as if they are sheep that have gone astray and need the assistance of a border collie to get them rounded up. Once all the little 'doggies' have been corralled, I break free from Kenny G. and make the following announcement.

> **And now, to dance their very first dance as husband and wife, please welcome to the dance floor _____.**
> **Music Cue: (example) 'Making memories of us' by Keith Urban**

At that time, there is a noticeable change in the mood of the hall. The bride and groom are on the dance floor all by themselves, locked in each other's arms. The relatives and friends surround them with their cameras and camcorders at the ready. They are in close proximity like the paparazzi and Brittany Spears. Someone in the corner turns off the houselights and I flip the switch and the music begins. Finally, as the music plays, I turn on my red and blue lights as well as my two banks of motion censor lights that move to the beat of the music. I turn on the multi colored disco ball, which sends colorful dots shooting out all over the room. The bride and groom normally pick out a soft, sentimental song for their first dance. I have many selections that are my personal favorites for this dance.

I'm getting a bad reception

I have the above-mentioned Keith Urban song listed as an example. Other songs that I like for the first dance are, *Could I have this dance for the rest of my life* by Anne Murray. That song was featured prominently in the movie *Urban Cowboy*. Other great songs are: *When I said I do* by Clint and Lisa Hartman Black, *I'll stand by you* by the Pretenders and *Endless love* by Lionel Ritchie and Diana Ross.

Nine out of ten times, the first dance goes off without a hitch. Of course, there is always that tenth time:

Eagles Hall – Gaylord, Michigan

It was an autumn wedding with a crowded house. The tables, which enclosed the dance floor before me, were teeming with enthusiastic wedding guests. Everything was going fairly well and the dinner portion of the reception was over.

I called for the audience to give me their attention. I called for the bride and groom to the floor for their first dance. Sometimes, clearing the floor is an arduous task. By the time you get to the first dance, the dance floor has been taken over by restless children. I have to spend a few minutes on the microphone asking them as politely as possible to move off to one side to make room. Sometimes, politely simply does not work and I want to hire a ringleader or a lion tamer. I was clearing the floor as assorted Mom's gathered assorted children, bringing in the sheaves at it were. By the way, what the hell is a sheave? Anyway, for some reason, the bride's father came up on stage and hovered over me. I forget exactly what he wanted but he made me nervous.

The bride and groom took to the floor and waited patiently for me to start. Dad was still hovering over me like the Goodyear Blimp at the Super Bowl. The music was all cued up and ready to go. Then, I pressed the play button on my DJ mixer. I saw the numbers on the timer moving and I knew the disc was playing yet I could not hear it. Absolutely nothing came out of the speakers. I had been playing dinner music for a while and I knew the mixer board was working yet it was as if I had played the *Marcel Marceau Greatest Hits Album*, no sound. Younger readers may not know that Marcel Marceau was a famous French pantomime artist. And remember kids, a mime is a terrible thing to waste.

I had a thousand eyes focused on me, their stares piercing right through my flesh like a warehouse full of knives. Those next few seconds seemed to go on for three weeks.

As it turned out, I merely forgot to flip on the microphone switch, so I corrected the problem and the happy couple took had their first dance as husband and wife. And my heart started beating again.

I never found out what the Father wanted as he stood over me and I got caught in his gravitational pull. A few weeks later I received a very nice letter from him, thanking me for playing and complimenting me on the fine job I did.

'You had people dancing all night, including some people who haven't danced in year,' was a sentence that sticks in my mind. I needed that. Every so often I pick up that letter and read it. It helps me prepare for nights like this:

The Ballad of Lex and Becky – or –
The Bride is high but I'm holding on

Wah Wah Soo Beach – Gaylord, Michigan

The wedding took place in July, I received the first correspondence with the bride and groom in March or April, this was a good sign, these people were getting prepared well in advance. Plus, they paid me the first half of my deposit, which was even better. Getting the second half would prove to be a wild adventure of its own.

I sent out the initial information packet as soon as that first phone call was made, hiring me. I take no chances anymore and I do not want a repeat of the incident with the flaky Jane Hathway wanna be lady from Grayling, who scolded me for waiting so long to get back to her. The information packet went out the next day for this wedding.

Within days I received the aforementioned deposit. I was given the check and only the first page of my agreement. I was informed that the rest of the paperwork would be sent to me at a later date. With a few months leeway, I was hoping the later date would be a few weeks before the wedding and not the night before.

I'm getting a bad reception

The cold winds of winter turned into the cold wind winds of spring. This is Gaylord Michigan in the heart of the snow belt of Michigan where on April 12th 2007 we had a blizzard, which closed school. Or was that a lizard?

Anyway, the glacier from Gaylord finally melted and it was quite a long time before I heard from anyone associated with the wedding. The frigid winds of April relented to the cool winds of May and shortly before Memorial Day I got a call from the groom.

I had not received the paperwork and I figured that he was calling to tell me to cancel the gig. Well we played phone tag for a few days and he finally got in touch with me. The gig was not canceled, he and his bride to be, lost the paperwork. They lost the paperwork that I had sent them several months before. Had they just lost it recently and called me shortly afterward? Or had they lost it several months ago and were just getting around to calling me about it? Time was running out at this point and we were quickly getting down to the wire.

As it turned out, he and the bride to be had recently moved and my paperwork got lost in the translation. He and the future missus lived down in Livonia, just outside of Detroit and had moved to a new apartment. I felt like I was talking to a spacey college kid, he sure sounded like one on the phone. If he lost my paperwork, was he going to be able to find his way up north for the wedding ceremony? Would he overshoot Gaylord and end up in Mackinaw City? I was beginning to doubt if there was even going to be a wedding ceremony.

A week or two later, the engagement picture for Lex and Becky (not their real names) was posted in the local paper. Lex looked like Superman's nemesis, Lex Luthor. Becky looked like Becky Thatcher from *Tom Sawyer,* complete with freckles and blond hair pulled back in a ponytail. In their engagement picture they looked like they were no older than about twenty- two. They were cuddled together and smiling and cute and charming, the whole nine smarmy yards.

About a month went by and the cold winds of May gave way to the artic coolness of June in Otsego County Michigan. It is hard to conceive of global warming when you have to turn the heater on in your car on Fathers Day. I finally received the rest of the paperwork for Lex and Becky's wedding. That was all well and good but there was nothing else, specifically a check for the rest of my deposit. I was beginning to think it would take an act of Congress or a crowbar to the wallet for them to cough up the rest of the money.

A week or two before the wedding, I got a call from Lex. After yet another session of phone tag, he told me that he and Becky wanted to meet me to go over a few things prior to the wedding. They also wanted to see all of my DJ equipment set up and ready to go so they could see what I was bringing to the party. The equipment is stored in the pole barn next to my house and I don't just have it set up on permanent display as if I were a club DJ. I have pictures of it in my DJ flyer and that is good enough for me. I don't know if those people thought I had some rinky-dink little Fisher Price music system or what.

I had things to do that night but I wanted to meet these two after all the phone calls. We agreed to meet at a local restaurant. It was on a Thursday night and I was coming off a busy 40-hour week of driving in crazy summer traffic in a busy tourist town. I work 7 a.m. to 6 p.m. Monday thru Thursday and by the time Thursday night at 6:01 p.m. arrives, I just want to go home and collapse. But I went to the restaurant and waited for Ditz and Daffy. And I waited and waited and waited for them. They were nearly two hours late.

Normally I would have had all the time in the world once I clocked out on Thursday, but not that weekend. On Friday I was driving my mother and myself down to see the musical *Wicked* at the Wharton Center Theater on the campus of Michigan State University. I had not even packed yet and I was wasting several hours wandering around the restaurant like a lost puppy, looking for the no show wedding couple.

I knew the names of the couple and barely remembered what they looked like from their engagement picture. I went to the maitre' de podium at the front of the restaurant and asked if anyone was waiting for me. They did not know me from Adam but they grabbed menus and offered to seat me several times. I decided to wait until the mystery couple showed up.

I roamed the dining room in the front of the restaurant. I then wandered to the lounge in the back of the restaurant. Then I repeated this journey several times. The restaurant was crowded with dinner guests and I felt like one of those spirits condemned to walk the earth for eternity, and by my watch it as going on half past eternity.

I'm getting a bad reception

I sat on a bar stool, a few feet away were three people, two of whom vaguely resembled the couple I was supposed to meet. I did not want to bother complete strangers yet on the other hand I did not want to be stranded in that restaurant until last call either. I went over to their table and asked if they might be the wedding couple, they were not, and I apologized for bothering them and went back to the bar stool and felt my blood pressure rising higher by the minute.

From the bar stool, I had a good view of the hallway and the ladies bathroom. I sat perched on the bar stool which was within a few feet of the ladies room and I think a few of them must have thought I was some pervert looking to score. I was merely a tired bus driver who had had a long day and was focused on the adjacent hallway further along that led customers from the front door of the restaurant, either right into the lounge, or straight into the main dining room.

I caught a glimpse of two people who I thought might be the tardy couple but I wasn't sure if it was them. I moved my tired carcass from the bar stool and as I got closer, I heard two people asking if the DJ was there, or words to that effect. I was right behind them and finally met the mystery couple. It turns out, Lex once worked at the restaurant where we met. The waitress asked me why I did not ask for them by name in the first place. I did not know she knew them or that he worked there or else I would have. I was a tired bus driver, not the Great Kreskin, I am not a mind reader. I was so tired and hungry by that time my mind was not functioning as it is.

We sat down and had some chitchat. Lex looked like a bubbly college boy. He wore wire-rimmed glasses and had an easy-going way about him. Becky never uncrossed her arms the entire time we talked. And when she talked or laughed her jaws were clenched so tightly you would have thought each breath would be her last. Becky must have had a problem with heavier people because her eyes never stayed on my face long enough to make contact with mine. The entire time I was talking to Lex, and trying to talk to Becky, her eyes were up and down on me like a bargain hunter scouring the racks at Wal*Mart on the day after Thanksgiving.

Lex explained he tried to get in touch with me on the cell phone to tell me that they would be late for our meeting. I am not allowed to use the cell phone while I am driving so there was no way to get in touch with me. They called my house and left a message but it did not do any good since I was not home all day to answer the phone. They were delayed for some reason and the traffic was bad and so on. They probably made a wrong turn coming out of Detroit and wound up in Toledo before heading north. It's possible.

We sat and talked for about an hour and I felt better having finally met them, and they felt the same way about me. Lex told me that his father-in-law to be was the one that actually hired me. Lex and Becky also told me they were afraid they might be getting some young kid as a DJ and they did not want that. I happily informed them that I have not been a kid since the Jurassic Period and I had about ten years experience as a DJ and knew what I was doing. I am glad I had a chance to meet them. I would have been even happier if they had handed me over the rest of the money, but that would have to wait. Lex was a laid back guy who was about to marry a woman who required a mechanic with a crowbar or a surgeon in order to crack a smile. Becky was a nice enough gal in her own way but she did not seem to be comfortable having the meeting with Lex and myself. God help me. And God help them if they did not pay me the next Saturday during the wedding. As it turned out, Daddy-in-law was paying for everything so princess and the frat boy could walk down the aisle. This was going to be an interesting party.

The following Saturday was a beautiful warm day in July. The wedding was less than a mile from my house. It was on the beach of Lex's grandmother's house. In previous correspondence with him, he gave me several locations for the wedding and I was beginning to think he did not know where the ceremony was going to take place.

The weather was absolutely perfect. The sun glimmered off Otsego Lake on a cloudless day. Boaters and jet-ski's sailed by, neighbors drifted onto their porches in curiosity at the goings on, on the beach that day.

I pulled up and parked and worked my way between a trailer on the left and the house on my right. The groom and his henchmen were getting ready in the trailer. From time to time, I noticed that as they drifted out of the trailer, they were passing around a large bottle of brown liquor.

Marvelous, they are starting already, I thought.

I'm getting a bad reception

I moved toward the lake and saw about fifty white folding chairs, split down the middle with an aisle leading to two steps and a metal archway covered in flowers that was sitting on the beach. The wedding crowd was dressed mostly in proper formal wear. There was a good share of the crowd however that dressed as if they were going to a luau. I wore a nice white shirt and a vest and a Looney Tunes tie, as well as nice blue church pants and dark shoes. Looney Tunes seems appropriate for many of the weddings I play.

I wandered around trying to get the feel of the place. No one knew who I was or what I was doing there. That would not have been so bad but I was carrying my trusty boom box, filling the air with Kenny G. His soft music made for a very nice mellow background for a wedding on the beach on such a gorgeous day.

Moments before the ceremony was to start, the groom had a last minute panic attack and looked as white as a sheet. He went into the trailer followed closely behind by his mother. A few tense moments later and both mother and son emerged from the trailer with tears in their eyes. I guess the mother went in to give Lex a pep talk or to threaten to kick his behind if he backed out now.

Kenny G. faded into memory as the Justice of the Peace walked down the aisle, followed closely by the clearly terrified groom. I started playing the *Trumpet Voluntary,* which let the bridal party know it was time for them to march. All members of the bridal party were properly dressed to the nines, except that none of them were wearing shoes, they were all barefoot. I suppose they did not want to get their shoes filled with sand during the service. Either that or they were already intoxicated and forgot they were even wearing shoes in the first place.

I switched over to *Here comes the bride* and Becky strode down the aisle in all of her freckle faced, clenched jawed, barefoot glory. I cut the music and the ceremony began. A loud boat full of revelers went by and I joked to one of the ushers who was standing next to me and said 'Let's make a note, next time, no paparazzi!' We both laughed.

The ceremony was over in just a few minutes and I played the recessional and split for the hall so I could set up my equipment.

I'm getting a bad reception

Livingston Township Hall – Gaylord, Michigan

Somewhere in the week that passed between our initial meeting at the restaurant and their wedding, Bex and Lecky, I mean, Lex and Becky underwent a Dr. Jekyll and Mr. Hyde transformation. Lex was just this laid back guy with a soul patch on his chin, at the wedding the patch was gone and he had this nervous intensity about him. He looked like he was so high strung he could have shot fire out of his eyes. He went from friendly at the restaurant to testy at the reception. Becky revealed her true self as this angry ice princess. She never cracked a smile the entire night and every so often, when she could lower herself, she came over to me and barked out an order and left. The two of them spent most of the night hanging around outside smoking with the bridal party.

It was a nice warm night and people did not want to hang around inside. A few tables away from mine, was a friend of the family dressed, as I mentioned, for a luau. He apparently knew Bex and Lecky from way back. He must have thought he was the official liaison from the bride and groom to me. He did not like the music I was playing and kept wanting me to change it. At one point he wanted me to play some Rastafarian music to get the party going. He made it point to tell me that I was losing the crowd and the music made everybody go outside. I told him that they couldn't smoke in the hall and that is why they were all out there. He came over to me every so often and informed me that the bride and groom wanted to hear this that and the other. If I put on something else he was right in my face and I really wanted to punch him by the end of the night. He should have gone to a luau and left me alone. Lex told me that he liked odd songs that were probably not appropriate for the wedding, and I think his annoying friend like the same music.

Lex and Becky had their first dance to an alternative rock song called *This year's love* by an artist named David Gray. I had never heard of him but once again I was lucky enough to find it on I – Tunes. Becky chose as her bridal party dance, some raunchy song called *Milkshake* where the singer wonders how her milkshake tastes or words to that effect. Lex also requested the Jimmy Buffet song, *Why don't we get drunk and screw* for the bride and groom's second dance. Classy.

90

I'm getting a bad reception

The groomsmen were hoisting large individual half pitchers of beer and most of the people who were at that wedding were drunk off their collective posteriors right away. The bride got nastier throughout the night and the bridal party got more annoying.

One guy from the bridal party would wander over and insist that I play either Jimmy Buffet or Neil Diamond all night. I would play one or two of each. Someone else would shoot across the room and insist that I take off that song and play something else. And then someone else would come over and not like either of those choices and insist I play something else. It was a frustrating night because I was damned if I did and damned if I didn't. More on this in the next chapter.

Long about ten-thirty the bride staggered over to me and I think she said 'I wanna do the dollar dance.' At least that is what I think she said because of the eight syllables in that sentence, she slurred six of them.

So we did the dollar dance, or in this case, the Dullard Dance, and those that were able to walk, participated.

Soon after that, the bride, who drank enough to empty Lake Michigan, was so drunk she had to be helped off the dance floor by at least four people.

Around ten after eleven, the bride's mother and father walked bashfully hand in hand, over to me and with equally clenched jaws said in a low voice, 'You are shutting this party down at eleven thirty. They are all drinking too much and it's getting out of control.'

Hallelujah

The bride's mother and father looked deeply embarrassed that Kitten was such a lush at her own wedding. They had paid for most of it and I am sure they were not too happy that things turned out the way they did.

I can just imagine Lex and Becky someday showing their kids the photos from their wedding album.

'Look Billy, this is where Mommy and Daddy got married on the beach and didn't wear any shoes.'

'This is where Mommy and Daddy had their very first dance'

'And this is where Daddy held Mommy's head so she wouldn't puke on her wedding dress.'

'And here's the phone number for Alcoholics Anonymous.....'

I still had not been paid the other half of my money and I managed to talk to the mother of the groom. She set the ball rolling and within minutes I got a hastily written check and several apologies from Kitten's mother. In all of the chaos of the day, paying me had slipped their minds. Well it had not slipped my mind and I was going to get the rest of my deposit if I had to lie down in front of their car in the parking lot.

When Kitten's mother handed me the cheek she seemed even more embarrassed and clench jawed than she did when she announced that she wanted me to shut the party down. The bride and groom and the bridal party consumed enough beer to quench the thirst of everyone in three counties. They all eventually disappeared into the night and I assume they all got home because I did not see any drunken idiots lying in a ditch along the highway. The parents had nothing but compliments about my playing and were very nice to me, possibly as a concession for the way the youngsters acted.

I was never so happy to see a wedding reception come to an end as much as I did that night.

Cut to October 2007, I bumped into the mother of the groom and I asked how 'the kids' were doing and if she saw them say 'Hi' etc. The mother of the groom informed me that Becky had a bun in the over, a bun that started baking on that warm night back in July. Becky was set to graduate in May 2008 and have the baby in April 2008. It's going to be hard to breast feed and walk up to get her diploma at the same time.

I learned that Lex was a history teacher and Becky was just finishing up her graduate work for a degree in Sociology. I humorously thought to myself that her Masters thesis must have been 'The effects of alcohol on horny women on their wedding night.'

11

The Bridal Party Dance – or –
With friends like this I could use enemas

Bridesmaids and ushers have their roots in Roman law, which prescribed that ten witnesses be present at a wedding to fool evil spirits who, it was believed, were in attendance at marriages with the purpose of causing mischief and disharmony. The bridesmaids and ushers were instructed to dress identically to the bride and groom, in order to confuse the evil spirits who presumably would then not know who was really getting married.
-----From 'www.hudsonvalleyweddings.com

If you have ever seen the We TV cable network reality show – *Bridezillas* you might think the primary duty of the bridesmaids is to kiss the brides ass, while resisting the temptation to knock her on it.

Outside of my initial contact with the client I don't normally see the months of planning and chaos leading up to that special wedding day. By the time anyone even remotely involved with the wedding ever sees me, at the ceremony or the hall; they have been through the wringer and are ready to party.

In my estimation, depending on how much work is assigned to them by the bride, the bridesmaids don't have an easy time of it. As far as I know the bridesmaids have to pay for their own dresses, which they will probably never wear again. Plus they all have to wear the same exact style, while trying not to look like the Lennon Sisters from *The Lawrence Welk Show*. And depending on the disposition of the bridesmaids, they can either be a barrel of laughs during the reception, or a colossal pain in the rump. Aside from standing up at the altar as a witness to the wedding, and of course getting to eat dinner first, I have often wondered what exactly the bridesmaids were supposed to do. So I looked it up on the internet and found the following:

Q: What Is The Function Of A Maid Of Honor? A Bridesmaid?

A: *The maid of honor (or matron of honor if she is married) has many responsibilities -- all of them fun, and all of them an honor (hence the title). She traditionally hosts the bridal shower (although if she is unable to do so, another bridesmaid or friend of the family may host), and may also organize the bachelorette party if there is to be one. On the day of the wedding, the maid of honor will help the bride dress, and basically assist in any way necessary. One of the most important things the maid of honor does is to stand beside the bride during the ceremony, and hold her bouquet when necessary. She is also the "keeper" of the bride's train throughout the day, from adjusting it when the bride arrives at the altar, to assisting with the bustle before the reception. The maid of honor may be asked in advance to give a toast at the reception, which will take place after the best man has given his. In some instances, the bride may choose to have two maids or matrons of honor, which is perfectly fine, and allows the two honor attendants to divide the responsibilities as well as the joy of being asked.*

Bridesmaids stand up for the bride during the ceremony, and attend the pre-wedding events. They also participate in the receiving line and assist the bride as requested at the reception.

-----*From TheWeddingChannel.com*

I'm getting a bad reception

Years ago I attended the wedding of a dear friend. Without exaggeration, she must have had between 25 and 30 people with her up there on the altar. This did not include the minister, the organist or the photographer. In fact I think there were more people standing at the front of the church than were seated in the rest of the church. The head table at the reception took up an entire wall of the hall and looked as if Divinci's *The Last Supper* had experienced a population explosion.

I have seen a few bridesmaids who have had an entire list of things they needed to get done before the wedding. Their mission, should they choose to accept it, was to get their assigned duties done on time, or before the bride has a meltdown, whichever comes first.

At the appropriate time, I will call the bridal party onto the floor for their special dance.

> **Bridal Party dance:**
> **Matt: At this time, please welcome to the floor, the ladies of the bridal party and their escorts for the bridal party dance.**
> **Bridesmaid_____Escorted by_____**

Once the formal part of the evening is over, I have seen waves of relief wash over the faces of many countless bridesmaids. At that point I get the music cranked up and it is not long after that when the waves of requests come pouring in as well.

I will be over in the corner at my DJ table, with dancers on the floor, when out of nowhere, a bridesmaid wanders over to me and makes a request. With several thousand songs in the catalog I can honor most requests on the spot. However at every party that I have ever played, somebody somewhere will undoubtedly say to me 'Do you have Such and Such by So and So?' And out of a quarter million songs on 700 CD's, I look in my songbook and don't have that particular song.

On the other hand, if I do have that one song by So and So, it never fails that they will ask for some other obscure selection by So and So. Apparently So and So is more popular than I realized.

I let the bridesmaids look through my book and normally they find something else they want to hear and I happily oblige. Then they go away for a little while until the next request.

Then there are the bridesmaids who have taken it upon themselves to be the official spokesperson for the bride. This is usually when the bridal party and several friends twice removed are outside smoking. The bridesmaids will appear like 7 year cicada's and insist that 'The bride wants you to play _____.'

Then why the hell didn't the bride come over here and tell me herself? I thought.

Then I will get a request for some obscure heavy metal or rap song that I have never heard of and I don't have. Then when I tell them that I don't have the song they look at me like I am a feeble old man of 92 instead of the occasionally feeble minded middle aged man that I am at 46.

I had one uptight little bridesmaid with an expensive hairdo, several drinks in her and one in her hand who asked me 'Do you have the song *Crazy Bitch?'* by the group Buck Cherry.

So I told the woman, 'No, I don't have *Crazy Bitch,'*

I thought, but I have a feeling that I am talking to one right now.

And then there is the Best Man and the Groomsmen.

Q: What Is The Function Of A Best man? A Groomsman?

Have you ever wondered about the purpose of groomsmen? Legend has it that this came about during ancient times when women were in short supply and a man had to literally kidnap his bride from her village, clan or tribe. The groom-to-be would bring along his 'best men' to help fight off angry family members or from competing suitors.

The best man of days-gone-by was responsible for more than the wedding ring. Since there remained a threat of the bride's family attempting to forcibly gain her return, the best man stayed by the groom's side throughout the marriage ceremony, protecting the bride and groom from any threats. He also served as a sentry outside the newlyweds' home.

I'm getting a bad reception

It is believed to bring good luck to the groom if the best man arranges for the groom to carry a good luck charm in his pocket on his wedding day. It is also considered good luck for the best man to pay the officiants fee in an odd sum.

Nowadays, the role of the groomsmen and best man are honorary positions.

-----From TheAmericanWedding.com

Years ago at a different friends wedding, the groom's brother was the Best Man. He had a veritable filing cabinet full of envelopes tucked into the pocket of his tuxedo jacket. Each of the envelopes was marked with a certain time when the Best Man was supposed to do something. There were such things as '7:30 – Toast the Bride and Groom.' '8:00 – Tip the bartenders.' '8:30 – Tip the band. Etc.' I've never seen anything like that before or since but the reception went off without a hitch.

Like snowflakes, no two flakes at a wedding reception are exactly alike. There are also no two wedding receptions that are exactly alike either. That is what keeps being an occasional wedding DJ from becoming boring.

For example, at the aforementioned wedding reception for Lex and Becky, Lex wanted me to have a groomsmen dance. I had never had a groomsmen dance before but it was his dime so I figured, why not. Truth be told it was his new father-in-law's dime but why quibble.

The formal dances were over and I called all of the groomsmen to come out onto the floor. They did not exactly looked thrilled about it. They were either embarrassed to do the dance or mad because they had to put down their barn silo sized beer steins for five minutes so they could dance.

Once the groomsmen got out onto the floor I played the (Groom) requested song *'Glory Days'* from Bruce Springsteen. The groomsmen stood in a circle and bobbed up and down and back and forth. White people not only can't jump, some of them don't dance very well either.

Once the dance was over, the groomsmen retreated to the bar or outside to smoke. Except for one particular groomsman at the dreaded wedding of Lex and Becky.

I'm getting a bad reception

I would venture a guess that he was in his early thirties. He wore the obligatory tuxedo and I think he had his beer stein surgically attached to his right hand. He had dark curly hair and a beard that looked like and overstuffed Brillo pad. Somewhere deep in the fur on his face, were two deep dark squinty eyes peering out. His beard reminded me of my one and only attempt at growing one back in 1995. It was not a good beard and I looked like the bastard child of Charles Manson and Grizzly Adams. Not good.

That was the groomsman who really liked Jimmy Buffet and Neil Diamond. Every so often he wandered over to my table and would yell out 'Jimmy Buffet, nothing but Jimmy Buffet all night long, WHOOOOOO!' That was all fine and dandy but regretfully I don't have any Jimmy Buffet in my catalog. One time, the furry groomsman stood glaring at me with those beady little eyes and said 'Jimmy Buffet, play it now.' I had to consult my *Drunk to English Dictionary* to try and convince him that I did not have any Jimmy Buffet. The next time he came over to me he requested *Forever in blue jeans* and many other Neil Diamond songs, those I have in my catalog in abundance.

After a few Neil Diamond songs, CB (The Crazy Bitch gal) swooped in to demand that I play something else. Fuzzy Wuzzy (with the Brillo beard) came back to me to demand that I play 'Jimmy Buffet.' This fun continued for a few more minutes and my next guest, after CB and Fuzzy Wuzzy, was dressed for a luau in a beige Hawaiian shirt and khaki shorts. Louie Luau as he shall henceforth be known, demanded that I play some far out, hemp inspired alternative reggae tune that I not only didn't have in my collection, I had never heard of before.

For quite awhile there was a battle of control for the DJ between CB, Fuzzy Wuzzy and Louie Luau. Added to the mix were the old reliable guests with requests and questions that I have seen and heard at every wedding. The faces are always different but the questions are the same.

'Could you speed the music up a little – play something faster.'
'Could you slow it down a little?'
'What do you mean you don't have anything from Eminem?'
'Take off this song and play something else.'
'Is this all the music you have?'

98

I'm getting a bad reception

'If we brought in a CD of ours would you play it for us?'

As I said I am usually the last of the wedding personnel that anyone sees after weeks of dealing with tux rentals, dress fittings, orders and chores and florists and banquet halls and caterers and ministers. I can understand that a lot of work goes into a wedding and by the time they get to me, the bridal party is ready to cut loose.

So I dutifully stand at my DJ table and suffer fools gladly, and as I do I know full well that I have given the people a night full of fun and music. Some of the music they like, some of the music they don't, but I have learned that I can't please everybody.

And as the night wears on and the booze kicks in, the cavalcade of annoying bridesmaids and groomsmen dwindles down to a precious few. I know that these people are an inevitable part of a wedding reception and if I didn't like being a DJ so much I wouldn't do it. So I take it in stride. I take pride in a job well done and rejoice in the fact that I only have to spend six or seven hours with these people and not the rest of my life.

And as I drive home, clear headed and sober and fully functioning I smile and I thank the good Lord that I never have to see any of these people ever again in my life.

12

The Father Daughter Dance – or –
My heartburn belongs to Daddy

Immediately after the bridal party dance, I keep the momentum going by making the following announcement:

> **Father/Daughter dance:**
> **Matt: And now for the Father – Daughter dance, may we please have (Bride) and her father (Father) on the floor for this very special dance.**
> **Music Cue: (Example) 'Daddy's hands' by Holly Dunn**

The Father/Daugher dance is a big emotional milestone of the evening. Father is done up in his tuxedo. The bride is done up in her gorgeous wedding gown. They are alone on the dance floor staring into one another's eyes as a thousand other eyes hone in on them.

I started as a DJ right when the song *Butterfly kisses* from Bob Carlisle came out. This song is beautiful and heartfelt, but it is so sickening and sweet that innocent bystanders may succumb to diabetes before the song is over. I haven't played it in a long time and thankfully other songs have taken over as the father daughter dance. *Butterfly kisses* is not really a bad song but it is just a little too precious for my taste.

A few songs that have replaced the dreaded *Butterfly kisses* have been: *Hero* by Mariah Carey, *Dance with my father* by Luther Vandross and a favorite of mine, the above mentioned *Daddy's hands* by Holly Dunn and *Daddy's girl* by Red Sovine.

Strife with Father

I played a wedding at the local Knights of Columbus Hall when I was still pretty new at this DJ business and wet behind the ears. I have a lot more confidence now but every DJ has to start somewhere. Even the legendary Wolfman Jack had to have a first day on the job.

The bride had everything well planned out in a detailed itinerary. She had a complete schedule of everything from the rehearsal, rehearsal dinner, to a timetable for the arrival of the flowers and cake at the hall. She had the wedding day planned out to the minute. She did a pretty thorough job. However she had nothing written down about her father. Such as how to avoid him or ignore him, and with what frequency he would come over to the DJ stage to harass me.

Everything was fine until Daddy dearest began his campaign of annoyance. The bride's father wore the usual tuxedo. He looked a little like Yul Brynner and had a Polish accent straight out of Krakow.

At the time I did that party, I was still using a home stereo with a small public address system and a small speaker that didn't carry well. Another problem was the hall itself. It is one of the larger halls in Gaylord and the dance floor is pretty big and the stage feels like it is two miles from the audience. No one could hear me unless they practically sat at or even on, my feet. So naturally Yul Brynner's body double came over to me every few minutes to inform me that no one could hear me.

'We cannot hear you. Speak louder.'
So I turned it up as loud as I could,
Father Superior sauntered away.
Then he sauntered back.
'You play music while we eat.'
Father Superior sauntered away.

Saunter back again.

'You don't know what you're doing. You are supposed to call the tables for dinner.'

What am I supposed to call them? I thought.

When the joy that was dinner was over, Daddykins held court with a bunch of his cronies at a table nearest the bar. He sat there holding court like Hugh Hefner at the Playboy Mansion. I never saw him sit with his wife.

I finally called dinner tables, as best I could, then I threw on some dinner music. I thought I was finally shed of Father Flanagan. But I was wrong.

When dinner and the formal dances were over I cranked up the faster music for the rowdier portion of the night, and things started going a little smoother. Then, just when you thought it was safe to go back to the dance floor, he struck again. It might help to read that last paragraph with the theme from *Jaws* running through your head.

Daddy came back.

I was right in the middle of a good set of fast music. He came up on stage and hovered over me like a giant redwood.

'May I help you?' I asked.

'I want to hear a waltz. You play waltz now!' I looked out on the dance floor and into the crowd and none of those people looked like they wanted to hear a waltz.

'What are you waiting for? You play waltz now.'

It was like a visit from the Soup Nazi from *Seinfeld.*

I should have said 'No waltz for you.'

As it was, at the time I did not have very many waltzes or polkas in my catalog. I have tons of them now but when the library was smaller I simply couldn't accommodate him.

I didn't have a waltz but I wanted to say something to make him go away. I was thinking about getting a clove of garlic and a wooden stake, but I said 'I'll look and see if I have one.'

Surprisingly he was okay with that and went away, for a moment. 'I'll look and see if I have it' has become my standard line for most of the parties I have played over the years. Most of the time it works.

I don't think anything short of a restraining order could stop the bride's father. At one point in the evening, he escorted a lady from the table where he was sitting, up to the stage to see me. Daddy wanted to hear his barfly sing a song.

I did my best to explain that I don't have karaoke equipment.

'But I wanna sing a song' chirped the barfly.

And I wanna point you in the direction of the nearest AA meeting, I thought.

'What do you want to sing?' I asked.

'What do you suggest?' she burbled.

I suggest you get off the stage and let me get back to playing music. I thought.

I was beginning to think that the bride's mother and father weren't married. They didn't spend a lot of time together. And Daddy seemed a lot more pre occupied with his boozy floozy and his bar buddies at the table by the bar.

Daddy stood next to his friend to make sure I let the woman dazzle the crowd with her singing talents. Eventually she sang *Slow hand* by the Pointer Sisters. She sang it directly to Daddy and mumbled as she sang. I turned it up as high as I could but the crowd was talking over her so loud they couldn't hear a note she sang. She acted as if she had just won *American Idol* and was wildly applauded by the Circle of Lush over by the bar.

I guess Daddy felt he had me in the palm of his hand. His visits were more frequent and more annoying. Finally I broke free from the confines of the stage and went over to the bride's mother and pleaded 'Will you please get the old man off back?'

She confronted him and told him to cool it. The rest of the night went pretty well. Toward the end of the reception, the night was winding down and I saw Daddy, off to one side, looking like the day and several dozen Vodka and tonics had caught up with him. Either that or he was exhausted from putting his foot in his mouth all night long.

One never knows.

13

The Mother Son Dance
Mommy beertest – or –
Cutie and the beast

Q: Is The Mother-Son Dance A Traditional Dance? Should You Have One*?*

In some parts of the country, a mother-son dance is traditional; in others, it is purely a preference. If you decide to include this particular spotlight dance in your reception, should be treated similar to that of the father-daughter dance, with a special song selected by the groom for his mother. The mother-son dance should be the third dance, preceded by the wedding couple's first dance, and father-daughter dance. If you're both on the fence, and your soon-to-be spouse is especially close to his mother, then it would certainly be a sweet memory.

-----From TheWeddingChannel.com

And then it is time for:

The Mother/Son dance:
Matt: And now for the Mother – Son dance, may we please have (Groom) and his mother (Mother) on the floor for this very special dance.
Music Cue: (Example) 'Wonderful world' by Louis Armstrong

The Mother/Son dance is another emotional moment. There are usually tears and a few choked up observers off to one side. I have played many different songs over the years for this moment. In some ways this is a difficult dance to capture in song.

A few of them have been *Unforgettable* by Natalie and Nat King Cole, *Wind beneath my wings* by Bette Midler, and this is no joke, surprisingly, *The house at Pooh Corner* by Kenny Loggins. My favorite selection is *What a wonderful world* by Louis Armstrong

Mommy beerest a.k.a. Cutie and the Beast

At the time of booking, I get a deposit, which can either be half of my total fee or the entire amount. My customers have been good about paying me. There have been those rare occasions when getting paid is as difficult as hunting for unpainted Easter eggs in a snow bank. But those have been few and far between.

On one occasion I was all set up when I spotted the mother of the bride entering the hall. She hired me from the very first bridal show I did at Carters in early 1997. She wore a light blue/turquoise gown. She also had an, 'I'm losing my baby girl today' look on her face.

We made small talk and then she said 'I'd better pay you before I get too drunk and forget.' This was a woman who looked like she should have been teaching Sunday school, not planning the night's big bender.

The other memorable thing about that night was the vast difference between both the bride and the groom's family. The bride appeared to be a sorority princess who more than likely was the head cheerleader, star athlete and the sweetheart of Sigma Chi.

The groom's side of the wedding was apparently bussed in from Dogpatch. The groom wore a white tuxedo and his henchmen wore the requisite black tuxedo, and all of them wore red baseball caps. I didn't get close enough to see which witty saying was on each cap but I'm sure it had something to do with Hooters or being a Bikini Inspector. As I recall, not only did the groom and the groomsmen wear caps, every male on his side of the wedding wore one too. Ah yes, this was a match made in Hooterville.

Throughout the night, whenever one of the groomsmen wanted to get the attention of the groom (or another groomsman), he would let out this deep, resounding, guttural 'WOOOOOOOOOOOOOOO', at the top of his lungs, from across the room, next to the groom or out in the parking lot. This was done while carrying a large mug of beer. As a casual observer standing off to one side it looked and sounded like some bizarre mating ritual on the Serengeti.

As this parade of fools strode past me, things got even wilder. Across the hall from me, a group of partiers were sucking down every last drop of alcohol in the bar. Most of them never came near the dance floor. One or two of them were even escorted out of the hall by the police.

Then, this glassy eyed young man who looked no older than 14 came over to me toward the end of the night with a few requests.

'Do you have any No Talent Screaming Banshees (Not the real name but it sounded funny to me when I typed it).'

'No I'm sorry I don't'

'Do you have any Wu Tang Clan?'

I stood there for a moment with a blank expression on my face and started to feel like an old fart.

'No I don't have any of them either.'

'Well what kind of music do you have?'

'What kind of music do you want? I've been up here playing for seven hours?'

He mumbled something and disappeared back into the group of suds suckers. I could see the disappointed looks on the faces of the sorority sisters and the farm boys in the crowd muttering something about the DJ but I couldn't have cared less.

Around eleven o'clock the bar tender shot across the room and said 'We're running out of booze so announce last call and shut down.' Those were orders I followed gladly. Rather than have a surly, blurry, potentially unpleasant mob on my hands, I made the announcement for last call. The partiers headed to the old watering hole one last time like bison on the lone prairie.

When the partiers finally stopped drinking and talking long enough to pay attention to somebody else, one of them asked 'Hey what happened to the music?' They asked this after I had quit playing for about half an hour and most of my equipment was put away.

They weren't the most observant group I've ever encountered. They also weren't the nicest. A few of them got belligerent, a few looked as sad and dejected as if they didn't get a pony for Christmas. I can safely assume that more than one of them felt like death warmed over the next day.

14

**The cake cutting ceremony – or -
Take this slice and shove it**

**Cake cutting:
Matt: And now in honor or (Bride) and (Groom) cutting
the wedding cake I have this special tune.
Music cue: 'Sugar sugar' by the Archie's**

*A wedding cake is the traditional centerpiece at the wedding
reception. You might find it interesting that originally, the cake was
not eaten by, but thrown at the bride! It developed as one of the many
fertility traditions surrounding a wedding. Ancient Romans believed
that wheat and barley were symbols of fertility and so, wedding cakes
included one or both of these ingredients. Incidentally, wheat was
among the earliest grains (predating rice) to be ceremoniously
showered on the bride and groom. In its earliest origins, the
unmarried young women attending the wedding were expected to
scramble for the grains to ensure their own betrothals, much as they
do today for the bridal bouquet. Somewhere around 100 B.C.E.,
Roman bakers began creating small, sweet cakes with it. The tradition*

of pelting the bride, or breaking it over her head, died hard. The Roman poet and philosopher Lucretius in "On the Nature of Things" ("De Rerum Natura") wrote that the throwing tradition mellowed into a custom of crumbling the sweet, wheat cakes over the bride's head. As a further symbol of fertility, the couple was required to eat some of the crumbs, a custom known as "confarreato," translated into "eating together." After all the cakes were used up, the guests were supplied handfuls of "confetto," a sweet meats mixture of nuts, dried fruit, and almonds.

The tradition of eating the crumbs of the wheat, sweet meat cakes spread throughout Europe. In England the tradition "broadened" to include the practice of washing down the cakes with a special ale called "bryd ealu," translated as "bride's ale," words that became the "bridal."

In the Middle Ages when food tossing became rice tossing, the once decorative sweet meat cakes evolved into small biscuits or scones. Guests were encouraged to BYOB (bake/bring your own biscuit) with them to the ceremony. After the wedding, leftovers were distributed among the poor. It is those very simple biscuits and scones that became the forerunner of the elaborate multi-tiered wedding cake we know today. Legend has it that throughout the British Isles it became customary to pile the biscuits, scones, and baked goodies on top of one another in one huge heap. The taller the pile, the more the future prosperity of the young couple, who exchanged a kiss over the mound. In the 1660's, during the reign of King Charles II, a French chef (unfortunately nameless) visited London, and, it is said, was appalled at the cake-piling ritual. It was his idea to transform the messy mound of bland biscuits into a beautiful work of art, an iced, cake.

The tradition of saving a piece of wedding cake is an old one, that some couples still hold to today. The custom is said to have originated with the concept that it was a sign of wealth for a couple to freeze the top portion of their wedding cake, thaw it out and eat it on their first anniversary. Most cakes don't freeze well for long periods of time, so couples wishing to practice this lovely tradition, should ask their baker to prepare a freezer-safe layer that will last the year in the freezer.

-----From www.hudsonvalleyweddings.com

I'm getting a bad reception

Take this slice and shove it

The cake ceremony is probably my least favorite part of the wedding reception. Nine times out of ten I get a good crowd on the dance floor and somebody will saunter up to me and declare 'It's time to cut the cake now.' At which point things usually grind down to a screeching halt.

So I stop the music after the current song I'm playing to announce 'May I have your attention please? At this time, So and So are going to cut that beautiful wedding cake sitting on that table over there. Now is a good time to get those cameras ready.'

This happens a few hours into the reception and I figure that by then, the guests have already walked past the cake several dozen times. In their hurry to get to the car the bar or the bathroom they may have walked right by it and never noticed. I think an empty glass or a full bladder causes temporary blindness.

By the time Aunt Bea and Uncle Ernie and several cousins to be named later gather at the cake with their cameras, it is getting closer to cake cutting time. Of course this has to wait, as several little children who have been running through the hall are shoed away from the cake table. I have seen many pieces of wedding cake headed my way with little kid's fingerprints in them.

Once the crowd control and the riot police are in place, I announce 'For this special occasion I have selected a special low calorie song,' then I play *Sugar Sugar* by the Archie's. This usually gets a good reaction, as well as some toes tapping from the crowd. A bride once asked me to play *When I'm 64* by the Beatles because of the line 'will you still need me, will you still feed me when I'm 64.'

As the Archie's chirp away in the background, the bride and groom join hands and stick a sharp shiny instrument into the unsuspecting cake with the skill of a first year surgical resident.

The precious first piece of cake is put on a plate or the palm of the hand or a napkin and the bride and the groom each get half of it. Some couples intertwine their arms and feed each other lovingly. Others choose to smash the delicate pastry into one another's faces, usually to the delight of crazed onlookers (what fun). Personally I think this is ridiculous. Putting on uncomfortable rental clothes and shoving expensive dessert into your loved ones face is as sensible as putting on formal ware, going to a fancy restaurant with an expensive buffet and shoving your loved ones face into the gravy, to the delight of crazed onlookers (what fun).

Although I think the cake in the face is idiotic, I'm not paid to give my opinion. If that were the case I'd have to charge a lot more than I do. So I put on my game face and laugh along with the rest of the crowd and pretend that a face full of crumbs and frosting is the funniest thing since the Marx Brothers. I even get on the microphone and say something like 'If you get a direct hit, they pay big money for it on *America's funniest home video's.'* Guffaw, chortle, laugh and giggle.

From there, either the bridal party or the bride's family are dispatched like the disciples to canvas the hall with slices of cake, making sure that everybody gets one. The cakes I've had have been delicious and the cake runners have always been kind enough to bring me one. There is nothing like a nice frosting buzz to set the mood for the faster dancing portion of the evening. If I am offered a piece of cake that I'm pretty certain has been 'kid tested', I'll respectfully decline. I don't know where those little fingers have been but I have a pretty good idea.

One bride even made the cake herself. It was lime green and had a smaller piece on top supported by plastic columns. Somewhere in the night, whether through the vibrations of the dance floor or the unbearable heat and humidity in the un-air conditioned hall, the top part of the cake fell like the stock market in 1929. Someone with skilled hands worked to build the cake to its original appearance but it was a losing battle. Back in the 1970's the narrator on *The Six Million Dollar* Man used to say 'we have the technology, we can rebuild him.' He didn't have a Hostess frosted snowballs chance in hell of rebuilding that fallen fiasco.

The cake looked funny but it was quite thick and rich, incredibly rich as a matter of fact. I think my blood sugar went well over 1000 that night. The bride served me up a piece cake that could have fed a family of four. She meant well but I think she put it on the plate with a snow shovel. The frosting was good but it had the consistency of spray foam insulation just before it hardens.

Another bride had the right idea. There was a smaller, bride and groom's cake that sat on top of four smaller columns about three feet high. Fanning out from the top level down to the table was tier after tier of cupcakes of all colors. It was a neat idea and the guests devoured them well into the night.

15

The bouquet and garter toss:
You don't throw me flowers, anymore

The bridal bouquet had its earliest beginnings, as a bunch of fragrant herbs who "job" it was to discourage evil spirits from getting close to the bride. It started not as a bouquet, but, with Greeks and Romans, as a garland of fresh herbs which the bride wore in her hair. In Victorian times, the flowers in a bride's bouquet carried messages, because each flower had its own special meaning.

The practice of the bride tossing her bouquet before she leaves on her wedding trip is said to have started in the 14th century, when getting a piece of the bride's clothing was considered good luck. In those days, the bride was treated poorly. Guests would grab at her wedding dress in order to tear off pieces of it. Although brides continued to believe they would not be wearing their wedding gowns again, they objected to its wanton destruction. Instead of allowing guests to tear at their gowns, brides found an alternative and instead, started to throw personal items, such as the garter, to the guests. Today, the groom removes and tosses the garter, while the bride tosses her bouquet. The unmarried man who catches the garter is asked to put it on the leg of the unmarried woman who catches the bouquet. It is said they will be next to marry (not necessarily to each other).

Yet another version tells us that the garter had a very practical beginning. When silk stockings were standard garb, this accessory was a necessity. This "version" of the customs origin tells us that the tradition of stealing the garter began in England. Young men took this pre-ceremony procedure quite seriously, as it was considered very good luck to "win the prize." To avoid embarrassing the bride, the custom evolved from stealing the garter into throwing the garter.

-----From 'www.hudsonvalleyweddings.com

If you have ever watched *America's Funniest Home Videos,* and really, how could you miss it since it is on twelve thousand times a week, there is a always a segment on weddings.

On video: At the wedding ceremony, someone passes out, someone barfs, has a crying fit or falls down. Very often this is the same person, but I digress.

At the reception, the groomsmen dance on a table and fall down. The bridesmaids over do it and they also fall down. Ashes ashes we ALL fall down.

Also on video: We see the bride tossing the bouquet. The single bridesmaids and other single gals are liked caged lions who haven't eaten in three weeks. The bride is the zookeeper tossing them a standing rib roast. The bride tosses the bouquet and the gals go berserk. It is as if the bride has tossed them the last available single man in the singles bar.

I have not encountered that level of desperation and pandemonium at most of the bouquet tosses that I have announced. At the appropriate time I turn off the music and call all the single ladies to the floor.

Bouquet toss:
Matt: And now it is time for (Bride) to throw the bouquet, we need all the single ladies on the dance floor at this time. So come on ladies get out those catcher's mitts and put on those running shoes, it is time to toss the bouquet.

Instead of mass hysteria there is a general apathy toward the whole sordid affair. And the gals that I have encountered at receptions would rather be outside smoking and drinking than chasing flowers around the floor or being pegged as the next Mrs. Whoever.

From time to time there has been a lack of single ladies in the house. And those that are, are not into the forthcoming frivolity of flowers. I have seen a few of them either head to the bathroom or out to the parking lot until the bouquet toss is over.

I have heard the dulcet tones of the married ladies in the crowd yelling: 'C'mon! You're single! GET OUT THERE!' I have even seen a few married ladies sneak onto the floor, impossibly hoping for something better. But this always ends with, 'You can't go out there! YOU'RE MARRIED!' Thank you, Mrs. Obvious!

Once we get all the single gals out onto the floor, I say the following to the bride.

(Bride) when I count to three, you let the bouquet fly. One, two, three! Go!

The bride lets the bouquet fly. I have never seen the crush of humanity or the leap of desperation that they show on those home videos, in the single gals that I play for. However when the bouquet gets caught, the lucky recipient proudly shows off her prize as if she caught the top prize in a trout fishing contest. There is cheering and applause and laughter. After the bouquet catcher has received her 15 seconds of fame, someone places a chair in the center of the dance floor, I call the bride over to sit on the chair and I announce:

Garter removal:
And now it is time for (Groom) to remove the garter,

The groom, depending on how far he wants to go with this, gets down on his knees and acts like he is diving into a pool of 100 dollar bills. The prized garter is there, all he has to do is reach in and take it.

By this time the bride is turning eight shades of red, the groom is as anxious as a hungry dog in a room full of raw steak, the crowd is hooting and hollering and whooping it up. There is really no better way to celebrate the sanctity of marriage than having your wife sit in

115

a chair, in front of your family and friends, while you stick your head up her dress.

But as I have said before, while I think this is tacky and played out, I don't get paid to offer my opinion so I put on my game face and say:

(Bride) (Groom) in honor of such a serious moment I offer you this serious song.
Music cue: 'The Stripper' by David Rose

As the music plays, the crowd goes wild and the groom goes in for the garter like he is trying to free trapped coal miners from a mine. I have only seen once or twice where the groom gets creative and pulls something besides the garter, out of the dress. I believe it was a big old pair of granny panties, and I think another time there was a license plate or something. If I remember correctly, another groom at another party went in with a flashlight or a miner's helmet. Classy.

Once the hunt for the garter is over, the bride and the chair are swept from the floor, and all of the single guys in the room are called to the floor.

Garter toss:
Matt: And now it is time for (Groom) to throw the garter, we need all the single guys on the floor at this time. So come on guys, don't be shy; it's time to toss the garter.

The women are genuinely more enthusiastic about the whole 'tossing experience.' And with the guys, well I haven't seen that much resistance to anything since the draft during the Vietnam War.

Sometimes it takes a great deal of coaxing to get the reluctant guys out onto the floor. When you've been holding up a bar stool or a good place out in the smoking area, you hate to give it up after all. Finally, when the guys are assembled and the groom is ready I say:

Okay (Groom) when I count to three you let the garter go. One! Two! Three! Go!

One or two guys from the pack will usually lunge for the precious garter, many times it is planned in advance, who is going to get the garter. The other guys in the pack hold back and avoid the incoming garter as if someone is throwing them a vial of highly radioactive weapons grade plutonium.

Up until a few years ago, once the hilarity of the bouquet and garter toss was over, I would resume the dancing. Then there was a wedding a few years ago when someone suggested that the gal who caught the bouquet should dance with the guy who caught the garter. This is supposedly indicating that whoever caught both items would be getting married soon. This struck me as rather silly, but in order to stretch this portion of the evening out just a little more, I began announcing:

> **Garter guy – bouquet gal dance:**
> **And now, the young man who caught the garter will place it on the young lady who caught the bouquet and they'll have their own dance.**

I could think of no better song for this crazy event than the following.

Music cue: 'Crazy' by Patsy Cline

In August 2007 I played a wedding where the garter and bouquet recipients just happened to be cousins.

'We can't do this, we're cousins' someone yelled.

'If it goes well, I'll name this the 'Cousins Dance' after you.' I replied to a lot of nervous laughter.

The awkward couple danced nervously together for a few tense seconds and broke free and went to neutral corners.

16

Tales from the dance floor

Beaver Creek Resort – Gaylord Michigan

The dancers my friend, are blowing in the wind

Dinner came and went and a few hours into the rowdier, faster paced, dance portion of the evening, ominous clouds rolled in and the sky got darker by the minute. It had been blue sky perfect all day long yet very hot and humid. The hall had no air conditioning and large window fans decorated the room along with crepe paper bells and streamers. It was the first week in June around eight thirty on a sticky Saturday night and it was still light out. As the dark clouds rolled in it looked for the entire world like somebody had hung a drop cloth on the sun since it got instantly dark.

The clouds were of the fast moving, rolling kind in a variety of dark and scary colors. The rain started and the wind came up. The hall was on top of the hill with an enclosed porch/balcony.

The clouds rolled and got darker, the wind and rain got progressively louder and stronger. The lights flickered off and on for a moment when someone got the brilliant idea to shout out loud that a tornado was headed our way.

There were about a dozen or so hyper little kids at that party and when somebody yells 'It's a twister, it's a twister,' pandemonium, screaming, yelling and chaos ensue. And it ensued all over the place believe me.

When the kids weren't scurrying about screaming they all took off for the stairs that led to the game room in the basement one floor below the party. I felt like I was playing on the S. S. Poseidon as the ship was turning upside down.

Short of handing out sedatives or pumping nitrous oxide into the room I knew I had to do something to calm the situation. I made an announcement that there was no tornado and that Dorothy and Toto would not be flying by any time soon. It turned out to be just a fast moving, yet loud, thunderstorm.

I announced 'As a tribute to the weather, I will now play the song *Stormy*' which I played immediately, followed by the song *Windy*. I thought it was funny and it got a laugh and the storm subsided rather quickly after that. That was one of my better parties.

Corwith Township Hall – Vanderbilt Michigan

Corwith Hall sits in the tiny village of Vanderbilt, about ten miles north of Gaylord. The hall has a distinct Northern Michigan look and whoever decorated the interior evidently got a great discount at Ye Olde Paneling Warehouse. There are no windows in the hall and when you walk in you might feel like you are trapped in the Brady Bunch TV Room. There is paneling up the yahoo. And if you have ever had paneling up the yahoo, you know how painful that can be.

One wedding I played there took place on an unbearably humid day in July. It was one of those days where the air was so thick you could have wrung the moisture out in a hand towel.

Several things stand out in my mind about that day. Normally the smokers take off to have their own party outside. On that day it was so humid that the air-conditioned hall was more appealing than grabbing a smoke. Those were the fastest smokers I have ever seen. No sooner did they step outside then they were instantly right back in the hall.

119

If I remember correctly, that wedding was the result of the bride having a bun in the oven. The groom looked as uncomfortable as humanly possible and for some reason never spoke a word to me all night. I had never met the bride and groom before that night. Many people meet me first, THEN don't want to speak to me. (joking)

The groom looked like he was 12 but was probably in his late teens of early twenties. He wore a white vest, shirt, black slacks and a baseball cap.

That was one of those parties where I got a lot of requests for harder edged music by heavy metal bands like Godsmack. I knew the musical *Godspell* quite well but Godsmack was foreign to me. And thankfully I didn't have any songs from them anyway. I guess I just have no appreciation for fine music. Please note the sarcasm.

I was hit and miss with the requests. Thankfully it was more hit than miss. If I didn't have such and such a song I played something else by so and so and they filled the dance floor for hours. It was a pretty good group to play for.

Someone came up to me and requested *Thank God I'm a country boy* by John Denver. When I played it, a bunch of my dancers took to the floor and did this wild and crazy square dance.

One guy wanted me to play *Alcohol* by Brad Paisley. Which was all well and good but at the time, I didn't have the song in my collection. He kept returning to me requesting that song despite my having told him at least 47 times that I did not have it.

'I'm not hearing *Alcohol*' he chirped.

So go drink some more and shut up already. I thought.

The food at that party was all home made and there were crock-pots full of steamy tasty goodness permeating the hall with a cornucopia of flavors.

In other words, the food smelled great.

Knights of Columbus Hall – Charlevoix Michigan

Then there are the parties where I cannot connect with a crowd even if I was covered in Elmer's glue, double sided tape and Velcro. This was one of those parties.

The hall sat just south of Charlevoix Michigan, a resort town about 40 miles northwest of Gaylord. I had only been to the lake Michigan resort town a few times. I had no idea where the hall was so I printed a map from the Internet and took a Saturday drive the week before the party to find the hall, which was no mean task.

I turned from US 131 onto a secondary road and would up at a dead end in front of a cement plant. I turned onto another nearby side road, which meandered directly into Fisherman's Island State Park.

Ranger Bob came over to me and asks 'Can I help you?'

'Yes, I'm looking for the K of C hall.'

'It's back down that road about two miles.'

'I guess I over shot it.'

'Don't worry, everybody does.' Said the ranger.

I thanked the ranger and went back the two miles to find a bland green metal pole barn that looked like a small engine repair shop. Had I not eventually found the elusive K of C Hall sign on the building I never would have recognized the place.

Cut to: A week later

To get from Gaylord to Charlevoix you have to travel on about 40 miles of a twisting, turning highway called M 66. There are not a lot of streetlights on the journey until M 66 runs into the small town of East Jordan and ends in Charlevoix. I was not crazy about running into Bambi or Thumper with my car on the way home so I went looking for a motel for the night.

No such luck. That was a big festival weekend in Charlevoix and every room was full and grossly over priced. So I had no other choice (short of sleeping in my car) but to take it slow and easy and watch out for eyes and antlers on the side of the road.

The reception itself was just, okay. I gave it my best shot but nobody really seemed to care if I was there or not. I played all the formal dances and the whole nine yards. But I could have been the music in an elevator for the response that I got. The people were pleasant but uninterested. They ate, danced a little and by ten o'clock the tables and chairs were being cleared. I began to think it was me but I know I did the best I could.

As it turned out, many out of town relatives and friends drove all the way to Charlevoix for the party and most of them could not find a room so they drove home early. Many of the guests had come up from the Detroit area. It is impossible to find a room up here on a busy summer weekend.

The mother of the groom said 'There were many people coming up but they couldn't get rooms. And believe me, the party would not be breaking up this early if more of our rowdier relatives were here.'

And it was too bad really because they missed a decent DJ and spectacular home made food. The mothers and the aunts and the grannies made enough food to feed every solider in Iraq.

There was a lot of sausage and kraut, meatballs, salads, bread and rolls and many desserts. Each time I walked by I heard 'Mr. DJ would you like some more so and so, we've got two or three pounds left.'

The party broke up early and I got home at an amazingly decent hour. And except for a large bat that flew close to the front of my car, the long dark road home was uneventful.

Livingston Township Hall – Gaylord Michigan

We're off to see the blizzard, the wonderful blizzard of ours

I played a wedding at good old reliable Livingston Hall on the first weekend in February 2007. The wind was very strong and the temperature that day never rose above a balmy –2 degrees below zero.

My DJ equipment is stored in a pole barn next to my house and under normal circumstances I can just pull up to the back door and load up. On that day in February I needed the services of an Iditarod team and an Eskimo to get my equipment to the car.

Despite the raging winds of winter, the party went smoothly. I did not see a lot of smokers lingering outside the door. If they were out there they were probably tempted to set themselves on fire just to keep warm.

One of the more memorable people I recall from that party was the bride's sister. She was a bridesmaid who came all the way from California for the wedding and spent the entire reception on her cell phone. It was none of my business but I was dying to go over and ask her who she was talking to all that time.

I'm getting a bad reception

Marsh Ridge Resort – Gaylord Michigan

Groom, despair, and agony on me

The bride and groom had several marriages and children between them. We had our initial telephone contact and the groom insisted on seeing my DJ equipment all set up and running. I am a mobile DJ yet some people think I must own a nightclub or bring my DJ equipment with me wherever I go. I explained to the groom that most of the time, my sound mixer and lights and such are in storage.

I got the impression that the groom fancied himself an expert on music and that everything I might have to say about it might not be good enough, oh joy, one of those. The groom was overly concerned about every note of music I was going to play that night. He must have thought I was some high school kid who had never played a party before. Maybe the fact that I look much younger than my age threw him off. Or maybe he just had a big huge stick up his butt, it's possible.

The party was at the picturesque Marsh Ridge Resort, located about a mile from my house. The resort has a great golf course and condo's, and a restaurant. The reception room where I played had a half dozen or so hotel rooms attached to it so the guests could stay and party all night and not worry about driving home. Somewhere along the line, they got the idea that I was going to stay all night as well.

The groom had every hour of the reception planned with specific things for me to announce or play at every turn. He mapped out the music he wanted, etc. I had my first actual sit down meeting with the bride and groom and they were very particular about the music and wanted to know everything but the kind and color underwear I was wearing to the party.

A thong and panties, you know, something tasteful without being gaudy, I thought.

'Church casual, a polo shirt, sweater and nice slacks.' I replied.

'Well what if it's hot that day?'

'The same, only without the sweater.'

I don't know what gets into peoples heads sometimes. People want to eat, drink and party, they don't really care how I'm dressed.

I'd never show up at a wedding in my after work, lounging around the house clothes. I do have more common sense than that. The focus of the day is on the bride and groom, not my BVD's.

Around midnight, twelve thirty, thereabouts, the party had been winding down for quite some time. People were either out on the balcony or out in the lobby sitting and smoking and talking. There was quite a span of time when I had nobody on the floor so I figured it was time to go.

According to the itinerary, the bride and groom were to leave around eleven. They didn't. It was much later. I was to make a goodbye announcement as they left, then I was supposed to play a last song for them by comedian Rodney Carrington. They would dance to that song then the adoring crowd would heap best wishes upon them and they'd be on their merry way. As it turned out the hall was seemingly deserted when the groom came up to me and said 'You can play that Rodney song now.' So I did and they danced and I thought they were gone.

Around twelve thirty a daughter of the bride or maybe the groom or both came over to me with a bunch of requests. By then I was starting to pack up. I told her 'No, I've been here playing for eight hours and I'm done.' She went running to the bride and groom to complain that I was shutting down. Another young lady who looked no more that 21 wanted to hear a song and I told her I was through playing for the night.

The highly intoxicated little charmer said 'You suck!'

To which I replied 'Well so do you honey!'

By then I knew it was time to go. The few partiers that were left were all sitting in the lobby. I think they got the idea that since they were all staying there all night I should too. That was never the agreement between the bride and groom and myself. And the bride and groom had not left the building yet but were hanging around shooting the breeze.

Most of my DJ equipment was in the car when I had my altercation with the drunk young woman who thought so highly of me. I was just outside the door loading my car and I could hear her in the hall complaining to the bride and groom that I was quitting and that I was rude to her.

I'm getting a bad reception

At first I was just going to slink off into the night but something clicked inside me that said I wasn't going to give that drunken snotty strumpet the satisfaction. I walked back into the hall with my head held high and made a direct beeline over to where the bride and groom were holding court. My number one fan was slumped over to one side looking all hangdog and depressed. I smiled and shook hands with the bride and groom and wished them well and they in turn complimented me on a job well done. We exchanged a few pleasantries. My critic looked like she was going to go and toss her cookies over by the nearest bush. Good! I smiled at her, and bid everyone a good evening and walked out of the winner.

Michaywe` Resort – Gaylord Michigan

Is that a bee in your bodice
Or are you just happy to see me

One wedding early on was held at the Michaywe` Clubhouse. This is the country club where I had my last encounter with Clara and the foundering singles club.

The country club and the golf course is set back deep in the woods and it is just as beautiful to take a ride out and look at as it is to play golf on. The clubhouse has a pool, a bar, an over priced restaurant and a split level reception area. On the south side of the building is a large porch. Continuing south from the porch is a pond with a fountain in the middle. Straddling the pond is a wooden footbridge which is ideal for picture taking. I am certain there must be countless photo albums from countless wedding parties posed for pictures on the bridge.

I played a reception at the clubhouse but I did not play for the ceremony, which was held on the adjoining porch. Evidently there was a bee problem (as opposed to an 'A' or a 'C' problem). The little guys had apparently set up housekeeping and built a hive under the porch. The groundskeepers had supposedly sprayed insecticide hither and yon to get rid of the bees. Someone should have told the bees.

During the ceremony the bride kept waving her hand over and near her bosom so often that it looked like she was having hot flashes.

The industrious little drone must have thought that the bride's cleavage would make a perfect hive for the buzzin bees.

The bride was nearly hysterical and the furious fanning of her front momentarily stopped the ceremony. In a loud whisper she called out 'There's a bee! There's a bee!'

The ceremony concluded without incident and the curious little critter flew away. It was another good party but I was concerned about some of the comments made by some of the hecklers in the crowd. I was still pretty new at the DJ game and I hadn't quite yet built up a tolerance for pinheads.

The bride's parents sent me a nice note a few days later which said 'You did a great job. Don't let those people get you down.' I needed that. Plus they sent me a nice tip, up and above what they had already paid me.

Well I'll be a son of a bee.

Northland Sportman's Club – Gaylord Michigan

There was another great party at a hall that was decked out in testosterone and road kill. I'm not a hunter so it was a little off putting seeing the walls lined with dead animal pelts, guns, bows and arrows and such. The food was great but I couldn't help but wonder if the main course hadn't been strolling around outside on all fours just an hour or so before dinner.

Seeing the skins on the wall reminded me of the Warner Brothers cartoon where Elmer Fudd sings 'Kill the Wabbit! Kill the Wabbit!' to the tune of Wagner's *The Ride of the Valkyries.*

Then I thought that if I did a lousy job, I might be the next mammal skinned alive with his hide nailed to the wall. I have left a few receptions feeling like I was nailed to the wall, thankfully that party was not one of them. It went quite well.

And besides, I don't look good in pelts.

I'm getting a bad reception

Super 8 Motel – Gaylord Michigan

MMMFlop

I played a wedding reception at the Gaylord Super 8 Motel. The party was for a friend of mine who I knew from the late and not so great singles club.

The party was right around the time when Ricky Martin was all over the airwaves, and his hands were all over himself with *Living La Vida Loca*. The other pop group of the hour was Hanson with their catchy yet hard to sing *MMMBop*. This was the song with the most indecipherable lyrics in pop music history since *Louie Louie*.

There was a group of teens and tweens at the party. When I played the dreaded *MMMBop*, they all sat at one table with their hands covering their ears. Well I can certainly take a hint (or a hike), and I announced 'Ladies and gentlemen, I have a special announcement. Due to popular demand, there will be no more Hanson played at this party for the rest of the night.' Applause broke out and there was rejoicing in Jerusalem, or at least in the meeting room of the Super 8 Motel.

This was the same party where the bride filled out my questionnaire and informed me on the 'songs you dislike page' – quote unquote 'My fiancé hates country music. So if you play any, we will stop payment on your check and you will not get any cake.' It was all in fun but I will never forget it.

Later in the evening, the groom's sisters started an endless stream of requests, all of them for country music, all of which were intended to drive the groom crazy. My allegiance at a party goes to the one who is paying me and I politely refused every request for country with the following 'He (The Groom) doesn't want me to play any country. You'll have to take it up with him.'

They were as persistent as moths on a porch light but I had my direct orders. So after about two hours of this musical dodge ball, the groom's sisters went and grabbed their sibling by the arms, dragged him over to my DJ table and coerced him into asking me to play a country song.

After a long, grim faced silence he grumbled 'Alright, play one, and that's it.'

So I played the *Watermelon crawl* by Tracy Byrd. What made this even funnier was that the groom was a rather shy, bookish fellow with a few big rowdy sisters.

Even later that night I played the classic Aretha Franklin song *Respect.* I got out on the dance floor and dropped to my knees and did the whole 'I'm not worthy' bit in front of the ladies. That was one of my better parties and it held a lot of fond memories for me.

And I haven't played *MMMMMBop* since.

Treetops Resort – Gaylord Michigan

I had known the bride for at least ten years. I was friends with her parents and a big group of us used to go tubing down the ice cold Sturgeon River south of Indian River Michigan. I had not seen them for several years and was amazed to see the bride as an attractive grown woman in her twenties.

The wedding was in June and I was hired the previous September. As time moved slowly from September to June, what began as a few emails regarding the wedding, turned into a blizzard of emails that rivaled the actual meteorological blizzard I described a few pages back.

First it was one or two emails a week, then one or two a day then it escalated from there. As it got closer to the date of the wedding I got scared to even go and check my emails. The bride had typed her fingers to the bone, not only to me but also to everyone involved with the wedding. The bride had plans and lists and itineraries and if there was even the slightest glitch I think her head would have exploded.

As I said I wasn't the only one involved in the blitz of orders and assignments. Her sister and her parents and various relatives were all lieutenants in the bride's army. Between typing emails and text messaging she must have developed quite a callous on her fingers.

A month or two before the wedding, I drove up to visit the bride's parents. What started as a simple get together became a planning and strategy session that rivaled America's pre war invasion plans for Iraq.

The bride's mother had a stack papers full of last minute details. What complicated matters was the fact that the bride and her intended lived 200 miles away. I imagine a lot of cell phone minutes being used up in preparation for that wedding as well as a few aspirin and several good stiff drinks.

This was the party out at the expensive golf resort where the pro's played, Treetops North. This was the wedding, which took place on the 18th green on a day when it was close to 100 degrees, and I (at the request of the bride) wore a three-piece suit.

At the rehearsal, my trusty, huge, RCA boom box performed like a champ. I played Kenny G, *Trumpet Voluntary, Here comes the bride* as well as the recessional; all went off without a hitch. It would figure that the next day, the CD player came down with PMS and skipped and popped and made hideous scratching noises and only played half a song at a time. I wanted to crawl under a big rock and hide somewhere.

As they say in the theatre, 'Bad dress rehearsal, good show.' My boom box bit the dust at the wedding but my regular DJ equipment worked great at the reception.

The party rocked into the night and I was only allowed to play songs on the CD's that the bride put together. I am really glad she put those discs together because it opened me up to a lot of great new dance music. At the bride's request, no one was allowed to make requests. That made this the first and only party in which I was not bombarded by requests. Later in the evening I played one or two songs that were not on the bride's itinerary and, given the way she reacted, I felt like I was being reprimanded for skipping school.

The bride's uncle fared no better and he was in charge of making all the announcements that night. Once the reception got into full swing there was so much rushing around and last minute preparation, as well as questions and confusion, I felt like I was back stage at the Academy Awards.

'How does she want this done?

'When am I supposed to say that?'

　　Etc.

It was a fuss and fury just to announce the bride and the bridal party but I handed over control of my brand new cordless microphone to the bride's uncle and he did a great job.

In some ways I wish all of my brides were as organized as this one was. In other ways, she had such a tight leash on everything (and yes I know it was her special day), that there was no margin for error.

I'm getting a bad reception

I got the distinct impression that while rejoicing and celebrating this momentous event, everyone involved was glad when it was over. I was happy to be able to check my email again without seeing 380 messages from the bride.

As the party was eventually winding down, the bride came over to me and said 'Matt, somebody said that I was anal. Is that true? Am I really anal?'

I stood there, looking directly into her eyes, and forced a fake smile on my face and lied through my teeth and said 'Why no, why would anybody say that?'

Waters Township Hall – Waters Michigan

The Ballad of Super Mario and Morticia

Waters Michigan is a one-horse town that the horse left years ago. It is merely a speck on a map which has two has two gas stations, a motel, a bar and a post office. It is right next to I –75 and used to have a Stuckey's, which closed long ago. In the early 1990's they built a McDonald's on the site of the old Stuckey's. That McDonald's had a pretty good shot at being the worst McDonald's in the continental United States. Service was dreadful and I think it was faster to go home and cook a hamburger myself than to order it there. The restaurant eventually closed and has been vacant ever since.

Waters Township Hall is a small meeting room with an adjoining hallway, across from which are a few township offices. The hall also has a kitchen, which smelled great when I got there to set up for the reception. Wondrous smells from slow cookers filled the air. I don't know how many guest were expected but the tables filled the small crowded room. There was no table set up for me so I set up my equipment on a table inside the coat closet. I can't count how many times that night a joke was made about coming out of the closet.

The groom looked like Super Mario from the famous video game of the same name. He had bushy black hair, eyebrows and moustache. He wore the usual groom's tuxedo yet not long into the reception he shed the jacket and shirt and vest and spent the rest of the night in the black slacks, suspenders and the unfortunately named 'wife beater' tee shirt.

I'm getting a bad reception

Morticia reminded me of Morticia Addams from *The Addams Family* and the wife from the family of groovy ghoulies that moved next door to *The Flintstones*. She had long black hair under a long white veil. She wore a vagina length wedding dress. If the dress were any shorter you would wonder if the bride had a beard. If the bride leaned in any direction, the mystery was over.

Upon request I play a special song for the bride and groom when I announce them for the first time, and they make they grand entrance. Super Mario and Morticia had a lot of furniture on their porch including a sofa and a washing machine. As a joke I was asked to play the theme from *Sanford and Son* as they walked into the hall. I found the song and played it at the appropriate time and it got huge laughs. Everyone including Super Mario and Morticia loved the song so much I was asked to play it several more times during the reception and I happily obliged.

Of course I had my contingent of smokers who spent most of the party outside. This group included one longhaired, Travis Tritt looking fellow who kept wanting me to play Ozzy Osbourne. I have several discs full of Ozzy now but I didn't at the time of that party. The drunker her got the more frequent his requests and the louder he yelled.

One thing I'll never forget was when nearly everyone there changed into more casual clothes. The bride and groom's family all changed. Then somebody got the bright idea to take a family picture and they all had to get changed back into their formal clothes, only to go back to casual a little while later. It was a sight to behold.

Another memorable thing was Morticia's request for a Marilyn Manson song for the bride and groom's first dance. I don't carry that artist in my catalog.

It was an odd crowd but they had a great time and liked me, they really really liked me. Toward the end of the evening a bunch of the party rowdy's acted out the entire *Bohemian Rhapsody* from Queen.

Once thing is true, being a DJ is never dull. Maybe despite of or even because of the mayhem and the odd characters I encounter, I like doing it so much.

The usual suspects

I have played many weddings in many different locations. One thing that I have discovered is that the names and faces change but the same characters are at every wedding, aside from the wedding party itself of course. A few of the more notorious characters are:

The Request Proxy – Adults who have been sitting at a table all night, spot a passing kid, either their own kid or someone else's, and send them over to my table every few minutes for requests. The adults never come over to me and directly ask for said request and they make the kid do the running.

One memorable incident with the Proxy took place at Treetops Resort in Gaylord. The bride was very strict with what music she wanted me to play, and any variation was absolutely not permitted. The uncle of the bride sent a kid up to me every ten minutes or so wanting me to play *Hair of the dog* by Nazareth. He did this to get under the bride's skin. I did not have that song and I would not play it even if I did. It got to be a little over done toward the end of the evening.

There was another wedding where the adults sent this little five year old boy over to my table to request the song *I like big butts and I cannot lie (AKA Baby Got Back)* by Sir-Mix-A-Lot.

There was another who sent a young man over to me with one request after another. He was a pre teen boy who finally said 'My aunt over there is a DJ and she wants to hear so and so.' The aunt was testing me by sending this kid to me every few minutes for one song after another. I passed the test with flying colors except for one or two songs. She even came over and talked to me for a few minutes informing me that she was a DJ and so on and so on. Big whoop.

The Scoffer – This is one who has been sitting at the table drinking all night and doesn't like what I am playing.   He or she is the one who will eventually ask 'Is this all the music you have?' This may also refer to number of CD's, lights, equipment, etc.

My fellow DJ – This is a relative who also does DJ work on the side and will inform me that he does his parties differently and with better equipment, lights, CD's etc. I often wonder why if this person is such a great DJ, why am I doing that particular party and he isn't.

The Admirer – One of the better guests at the wedding reception. The guy with the beer in his hand who comes up to me and just wants to shoot the breeze while flipping through my DJ catalog. This is the best guy to crack a few jokes with as we can both find something funny about the reception.

The Bar Fly - This is usually an older guy who is seemingly cemented to his bar stool and has not moved an inch except to eat and go to the bathroom. My dancers have been having a good time on the floor all night and Otis the Drunk will wander over to me after five hours and want me to play Merle Haggard or Johnny Cash. I have plenty of music from both of those artists so that is not a problem. The problem is when Otis gets irritated that I am not playing his request RIGHT THIS VERY MINUTE!!!!

The Outsiders – I have stated quite often in this book already that you cannot smoke in many of the halls that I play in. And most of the time I end up playing to an empty house. The smokers are standing just outside the door, listening to the music. I had one brilliant observer point to me and say 'There is nobody on the floor dancing so you'd better play something else. They don't like the music.'

To which I said 'They are all outside smoking, that's why they aren't in here.'

And of course I thought: Genius, it is not my music that sends them outside, it is the lure of Merit Ultra Light 100's and Marlboro's. You twit.

I don't smoke so the no smoking rules are just fine by me. Now if they would only come up with a no agitator clause that would be great. Of course, if that happened there would be no one at all to play for at most weddings.

After being a DJ all these years I play a little game inside my head called '*Spot the agitator.*' Which person in the hall who is somewhat civilized and well behaved now, will turn into a colossal pain in the ass or a thorn in my side later. There is one in every crowd but they are hard to spot right away.

The Designated Agitator – Much of the time, the DA, Designated Agitators, are little pre-teen girls who want some rap song or whatever song Britney Christina Jessica Beyonce' Pop Princess has just recorded and released five minutes ago. They get that sad little puppy dog look on their face when I tell them I don't have it.

I'm getting a bad reception

I can just imagine some of these people in ten years whining to a therapist about how their lives were ruined because that dumb DJ did not play *Whoop there it is* at Cousin Bootsy's wedding.

Last Call

The vows and rings have been exchanged. The dinner has been eaten and the cake has been shoved.

The children were nestled all snug in their beds, while visions of sugarplums danced in their heads.

 Sorry, wrong story.

The dance was danced, the feast was grand and the spirits flowed like a river. As the crowd dwindles down to a precious few, the tables are cleared and the dishes are put away and it is last call, time to go home.

Usually when I see an empty floor and small pockets of humanity nursing that last drink, I'll announce last call and wrap things up for the night.

Since I first began as a DJ I have always played *I've had the time of my life* from *Dirty Dancing,* sung by Jennifer Warnes and Bill Medley. In late 2007 I switched to the more obvious *Last Dance* by Donna Summer, followed immediately by *Goodnight Sweetheart* by The Spaniels. And then the music is over for the night.

What follows is a rather surreal moment when my flashing lights stop and the house lights come up in the hall. This reality check is amusing to watch when my revelers discover that the party is over. It is like Sheriff Andy Taylor trying to clear Otis out of the drunk tank at the Mayberry County Jail on Sunday Morning.

It is as inevitable as the sunrise that somebody in the crowd doesn't want to leave just yet. Some of them offer me bribes. One guy offered me twenty-five bucks if I would let him borrow my boom box so he and his buddies could have music to drink to. That was all well and good but I had never met the guy before and I wasn't about to play this little game with him. The odds of me ever seeing that twenty-five dollars or my boom box ever again were the same as seeing the Titanic sail into New York tomorrow. Besides it wouldn't be right to take money from somebody three sheets to the wind.

I'm getting a bad reception

I have seen crying jags to rival Tammy Faye Bakker on *The PTL Club.* At one reception, most of my equipment was already in my car and this bridesmaid turned on the waterworks. She was quite a sight.

'Waaaaaaaaaaaah! There's no more music! Why did he stop playing? Waaaaaaaaaaaah' She wailed and cried her eyes out.

'But the party is over and everyone is gone,' said the bride in a parental tone 'It's time to go.'

'Waaaaaaaaaaaaaaaaaaaaaaah! Sniff, sniff, bawl' Well you get the idea.

The soused bridesmaid sat in a chair, slumped over a table looking sad and dejected. It was pitiful in the same way a wet puppy is pitiful. I didn't want to laugh, at least not directly to her face so I chuckled all the way home.

And so, as I pack up my DJ equipment, I get in my car and drive home. I know that I have done my best. Some parties are terrific, a few have been awful, most of them are memorable and none of them are boring.

And if I ever get tired of bringing the music to the masses (and in a few rare cases, the asses), I am sure there is always a sequel to this book waiting for me out there somewhere. Until then, please enjoy the final chapter of this book, dedicated to those toe tapping tunes that keep my dancers coming back for more.

17

Top of the Pops

This chapter is dedicated to songs that I have played at nearly every party. Musical tastes come and go but the old stand bys are there at every reception. In fact I think it may be an unwritten law in some states that I have to play these songs in order to be a genuine DJ. These songs get such a great reaction that I am happy to oblige. And as long as I don't have to sing in public, since I can't carry a tune in a bucket, that's all the better.

Now before I go on, I know there is a multitude of DJ's who do things a million different ways. The songs listed here, in alphabetical particular order, are the favorites that worked for me.

Old time rock and roll

"Old Time Rock and Roll" is a song made famous by Bob Seger and featured in his 1978 album Stranger in Town. It is a nostalgic look at the music of a previous generation. The song was featured in the Tom Cruise film Risky Business and gained widespread notoriety because of its inclusion. The song was recorded at Muscle Shoals

I'm getting a bad reception

Sound Studios in Muscle Shoals, AL. The famous piano "false start" at the beginning of the song was actually an error caused by the tape operator at the legendary recording studio. Seger and his management, however, liked how the "mistake" sounded and kept it in the final mix.

Bob Seger's version is actually quite different from the original; said he in 2006: "All I kept from the original was: Old time rock and roll, that kind of music just soothes the soul, I reminisce about the days of old with that old time rock and roll. I rewrote the verses and I never took credit. That was the dumbest thing I ever did. And Thom Jones and George Jackson know it too. But I just wanted to finish the record [Stranger in Town]. I rewrote every verse you hear except for the choruses. I didn't ask for credit. My manager said: "You should ask for a third of the credit." And I said: "Nah. Nobody's gonna like it." I'm not credited on it so I couldn't control the copyright either. Meanwhile it became a Wendy's commercial because I couldn't control it. Oh my god, it was awful!"

Although Seger's version only reached number 28 on the U.S. pop charts when released as a single in 1979, it achieved substantial album-oriented rock radio airplay. A version of the song was released as a single in 2000 by Status Quo and featured on their Famous in the Last Century album.

In 2001 the song was chosen by RIAA as one of the Songs of the Century. On 30th November 2006 it was featured on BBC soap Eastenders with Gary and Minty dancing to the song on the radio.
--------wikipedia

All it took was Tom Cruise sliding across the floor in his skivvies in *Risky Business* to make this Bob Seger song a pop culture legend. In the film, Cruise plays Joel, an enterprising high school student who turns his parents' home into a brothel as part of a business class project.

Old time rock and roll has been parodied on *Saturday Night Live* when Ron Reagan hosted the show. He played himself in a scene where he was home alone while Ron and Nancy were away. It has also been featured in a Little Friskies Cat Food commercial called *Frisky Business.*

I'm getting a bad reception

I used to wait to play this song but now it is the first fast song right out of the box right after the formal dances.

While it is tempting, I don't slide across the floor in my underwear for any amount of money. I'll have to double my fee for that.

The Chicken Dance

The name of the original Swiss song was Der Voglertanz (The Bird Dance). Since 1963,Werner Thomas had played it in restaurants and hotels. During one of Thomas' performances, Belgian producer Louis van Rijmenant heard the song. Van Rijmenant made some lyrics and in 1970 released it to the public, without much success. In 1977, Dutch local band "De Electronica's" released an instrumental version, which became a hit, and started the international success of the song. On some recorded releases of the music Werner Thomas is listed as the composer, while on others other authors are listed, e.g., as "Thomas/Rendall/Hose", probably including the authors of the particular arrangement. Since then the song has become known under numerous other "birdie" names, including "Vogerltanz" (Bird Dance), "Danse des Canards", "Chicken Dance" and "Dance Little Bird". Over 140 versions of it are recorded worldwide, including Walt Disney Records, together making over 40,000,000 records.

In 1982 it was introduced to the USA on Nationwide TV's "PM Magazine Show", (GROUP W PRODUCTIONS) as the "CHICKEN DANCE" by Wisconsin Orchestra leader Norm Edlebeck. Despite other claims as to the name "Chicken Dance", the name came about because an Austrian tour guide translated "Bird Dance / Dance Little Bird" and other similar names, from German to English by calling it "The Chicken Dance" when Norm Edlebeck's Band appeared in Austria in the fall of 1981. Edlebeck recorded it on the "End of The Trail" record label and used his nickname "Whoopee" as the artist.

Contrary to some misconceptions, it is not an Austrian folk dance, although it was presented as one in the Austrian film Das Fest des Huhnes.

In the United States, the publishing rights for the song were acquired by a New York publisher Stanley Mills.

It has become popular in the USA as a German heritage song, and has been likewise adopted by people worldwide of many cultures since its creation. It has become a staple dance at weddings and at Oktoberfests.

Dance steps

The "Chicken Dance" song is accompanied by a dance requiring a group of people, and it goes as follows:

Begin in a large circle with everybody facing in toward the center of the ring.

At the start of the music, shape a chicken beak with your hands. Open and close it four times, during the first four beats of the music.

Make chicken wings with your arms. Flap your wings four times, during the next four beats of the music.

Make a chicken's tail feathers with your arms and hands. Wiggle downwards during the next four beats of the music.

Clap four times during the next four beats of the music.

Repeat this process four times.

After the fourth time spin to the right for eight counts with your partner.

Switch directions and spin to the left with your partner for eight counts.

The dance repeats, progressively getting faster and faster, until the music stops.

A common alternate beginning goes as follows:

Start with either a group of people (arranged specifically or not), or simply one or two people.

At the start of the music, shape chicken beaks with both of your hands. Open and close them for the first four beats of the music.

Make chicken wings with your arms. Flap your wings four times, during the next four beats of the music.

Bring your arms down, while bending your elbows at a 90 degree angle, and twist your body and your arms in alternate directions (as if performing The Twist by Chubby Checker). Wiggle downwards at the same time to the next four beats of the music.

Continue as previously described.

-----wikipedia

I'm getting a bad reception

Poultry would never be the same again with the introduction of the dreaded *Chicken Dance*. What is essentially a polka on a caffeine high has an equal amount of fans as well as detractors. I had one bride inform me that she did not want any 'dumb songs' played at her wedding, including the *Chicken Dance*. That's all well and good but if you take out all the so-called 'dumb songs', the wedding reception would have only been 12 minutes long.

The song has no lyrics that I know of but at one party, just for fun I called out the following to the beat of the music:

Finger finger finger finger
Elbow elbow elbow elbow
Butt butt butt butt
Clap clap clap clap

A more creative group of pre teen girls at another party made up these lyrics:

I don't wanna be a chicken
I don't wanna be a duck
So kiss my butt
(clap clap clap clap)

The Locomotion

"The Loco-Motion" is a 1962 pop song written by American songwriters Gerry Goffin and Carole King. Its initial release by Little Eva went to US #1. The song is notable for making Top 5 in the USA three times: for Little Eva (1962); for Grand Funk Railroad in 1974 (US #1); and for Kylie Minogue in 1988 (US #3). It is sometimes categorised as belonging to the '60s girl group sound (which Goffin and King helped create), though it was recorded by a solo artist.

Original Little Eva version and dance

The song is a popular and enduring example of the dance-song genre: much of the lyrics are devoted to a description of the dance itself, usually done as a type of line dance. The song became an instant smash, reaching #1 in the US in 1962.

I'm getting a bad reception

The artist known as Little Eva was actually Carole King's babysitter, having been introduced to King and husband Gerry Goffin by The Cookies, a local girl group who would also record for the songwriters. Apparently the dance came before the lyrics; Eva was bopping to some music that King was playing at home, and a dance with lyrics was soon born. It was the first release on the new Dimension Records label, whose girl-group hits were mostly penned and produced by Goffin and King

The Loco-Motion was quickly recorded by British girl group The Vernons Girls and entered the chart the same week as the Little Eva version. The Vernons Girls' version stalled at number 47 in the UK, while the Little Eva version climbed all the way to number 2 on the US charts. It re-entered the chart some ten years later and almost became a top ten again, peaking at number 11.

The Little Eva version of the song was featured in the 2006 David Lynch film Inland Empire in a sequence involving several characters, including lead Laura Dern, performing the dance routine. The scene has been noted as being particularly surreal, even by the standards of David Lynch movies.

Grand Funk Railroad version

Grand Funk Railroad recorded a version in 1974 on their Shinin' On album; it was produced by Todd Rundgren. Like the Little Eva version, it reached #1 on the U.S. charts.

"The Loco-Motion" was performed by Australian dance-pop singer Kylie Minogue on her debut album Kylie (1988). It was produced by Stock Aitken & Waterman, and received a mixed reception from music critics. The song, a cover of the Little Eva hit, was subsequently remixed and released as the third single in the summer of 1988 (see 1988 in music)and was a top five hit in the United Kingdom, debuting at number two, giving Minogue the record for the highest entry on the UK singles charts by a female artist, a record previously held by Madonna. It also reached number three on the U.S. Billboard charts with sales in excess of 0.5 million and made number one in Canada, giving Minogue three simultaneous number ones internationally.

Jerick's different version of the song was originally released by Minogue as her debut single on July 27, 1987 in Australia under the title "Locomotion". After an impromptu performance of the song at an Australian rules football charity event with the cast of the Australian soap opera Neighbours, Minogue was signed a record deal with Mushroom Records to release the song as a single. The song was a hit in Australia, reaching number one and remained there for an amazing seven weeks. The success of the song in her home country led to her signing a record deal with PWL Records in London and to working with the hit producing team, Stock, Aitken and Waterman.

The music video for "Locomotion" was filmed at Essendon Airport and the ABC studios in Melbourne, Australia. The video for "The Loco-Motion" was created out of footage from the Australian music video.

At the end of 1988, the song was nominated for Best International Single at the Canadian Music Industry Awards.

Trivia

The original Australian video to "Locomotion" was sponsored by Impulse, whose marketing was dropped from the UK version of the video, re-cut from the original. However, in both versions Kylie's brother Brendan is pictured in the final ensemble wearing a leather bomber jacket and jeans, though this is often overlooked given that her sister Dannii appears in her video for "What Do I Have To Do", an iconic track from her third album "Rhythm of love"

Chart performance

In the United Kingdom the song was released on July 25, 1988 and debuted at number two on the singles chart — the highest entry on the UK singles charts by a female artist — due to strong 7" single sales and radio airplay. It remained in the number two position for four weeks before falling to number three. The song became Minogue's third top five single in the UK and remains one of her most successful single releases to date.

In late 1988 Minogue travelled to the United States to promote "The Loco-Motion" she did many interviews and performances on American television.

I'm getting a bad reception

"The Loco-Motion" debuted at number eighty on the U.S. Billboard Hot 100 and later climbed to number three for two weeks. The song was Minogue's second single to chart in the U.S., but her first to reach the top ten. It remains her biggest hit in the United States. She would not even reach the top ten again until 2002 with the release of "Can't Get You Out Of My Head", which reached number seven on the chart.

In Canada the song reached number one.

In Australia the song was released on July 27, 1987 and was a huge hit reaching number one on the AMR singles chart, remaining there for seven weeks. The song set the record as the biggest Australian single of the decade. Throughout Europe and Asia the song also performed well on the music charts, reaching number one in Belgium, Finland, Ireland, Israel, Japan, and South Africa.

The flip-side "I'll Still Be Loving You" is a popular song, and one of the few not released as a single from her huge selling debut album "Kylie".

The Locomotion is another crowd pleaser. I have seen many crowds in many different venues gather and put their hands on the shoulders or waist of the person in front of them to form a line. Many times it is the bride who is first in line and gets the ball, or in this case, the train, moving. It is not unusual to see the train leave the floor and roam through the hall.

I have seen the train leave the hall completely and go outside only to return moments later through another door. At times I will pause the music where it was when the train went outside, then resume it at the same spot when the train enters the station. I have also see the line break into several smaller groups of people dancing by themselves scattered about the floor which looked like an Amtrak derailment.

The Love Shack

"Love Shack" is a hit single by rock band The B-52's. Originally released in 1989 from their album Cosmic Thing, the single was the band's greatest hit song and first million-copy seller. It was also the band's first song to reach the Billboard Top 40 charts, peaking at

143

number three, also reaching number two on the UK Singles Chart, and was number one for eight weeks in Australia.

Produced by Don Was, the song's inspiration was a cabin around Athens, Georgia, complete with tin roof, where the band conceived "Rock Lobster," a single from their first album. B-52's singer Kate Pierson lived in the cabin in the 1970s, and the cabin existed until 2004, when it burned down in a fire. The song acted as a comeback of sorts following the band's decline in popularity in the 1980s coupled with the death of their guitarist, Ricky Wilson, in 1985.

The song received a number of accolades following its release. Named one of the 365 Songs of the Century in a report by the United States Senate Subcommittee on the Department of the Interior, the video for the song received an award from MTV as the Best Group Video, and was named the Best Single of 1989 by Rolling Stone. Additionally, it was ranked #243 in Rolling Stone's list of the 500 Greatest Songs of All Time

In 1999, the song was parodied as "Glove Slap" in The Simpsons episode "E-I-E-I-(Annoyed Grunt)."

The song received additional notoriety in 2005 when United States Court of Appeals for the Eleventh Circuit Judge William H. Pryor, Jr. quoted the song in his majority opinion in a case regarding an ordinance blocking adult entertainment businesses from acquiring business permits. Judge Pryor referenced the lyrics of the song, "Huggin' and a kissin', dancin' and a lovin', wearin' next to nothing," in his description of the adult business involved with the case.

-----wikipedia

This is a great song that creates a party buzz from its first notes to its last. It makes you want to get a bunch of your friends together to go party and dance. The titular shack is not so much to look at on the outside but the music is hot on the inside.

It's fun to participate when the lead singer says 'Bang bang bang on the door baby!' 'Knock a little louder sugar – I can't hear you!' And it is fun to imagine you are driving the Chrysler (mentioned in the song) that is as big as a whale.

At the end of the song, every crowd I have ever played this song for really gets into yelling the somewhat vague coda of the song: 'You're what? Tin roof rusted!'

I'm getting a bad reception

It is an all around great feel good song.

The Macarena

"Macarena" is a song by Los del Río about a woman of the same name, or any woman from the La Macarena neighbourhood of Seville. It was very successful between 1995 and 1997.

The song became the second longest running #1 and best selling debut single of all time in the US. It was ranked the "#1 Greatest One-Hit Wonder of all Time" by VH1 in 2002.

As a result of their lounge act, Los del Río were invited to tour South America in March, 1992, and while visiting Venezuela, they were invited to a private party held by the Venezuelan impresario (of Cuban descent) Gustavo Cisneros. Many prominent Venezuelans were in attendance that night, including former president Carlos Andrés Pérez.

Cisneros had arranged for a local flamenco teacher, Diana Patricia Cubillán Herrera, to do a small performance for the guests, and Los Del Rio were pleasantly surprised by Cubillán's dance skills. Spontaneously, Romero recited the song's chorus-to-be on the spot, as an accolade to Cubillán, but naming her "Ma'dalena" (Magdalena): "Dale a tu cuerpo alegría, Ma'dalena, que tu cuerpo e' pa' darle alegría y cosa' buena'" ("Give your body some joy, Magdalene, 'cause your body is for giving joy and good things to"). In Andalusian culture labeling a woman "Magdalena" is to give her a faint association with Mary Magdalene's reportedly seedy past, and more accurately describes her as being sassy or sensuous.

Antonio Romero saw potential in the improvised rhyme, and back at their hotel the duo came up with the basic structure of the song. Since "Magdalena" was also the title of another song by Mexican-Spanish singer Emmanuel quite popular at the time, Romero suggested that they use "Macarena" instead, which — besides being part of one of his daughters' name; is a rather popular name in Andalusia, given its association with the Virgin of the Macarena, the incarnation of the Virgin Mary that is a patroness of Seville's barrio La Macarena. The Virgin-Magdalene dichotomy probably explains the rest of the lyrics: a song about a young woman, the girlfriend of a recent recruit to the Spanish Army named Victorino (whose name may

145

be inspired from a kind of bull with long horns, evoking the cornudo, or male victim of his partner's infidelity, a mental image common in Spanish and Latin American culture), who celebrates his drafting by hooking up with two of his male friends. Macarena has a weakness for males in uniform, spending summers at Marbella, and dreams of shopping at El Corte Inglés (the major Spanish department store chain), moving to New York City and getting a new boyfriend.

The song was originally released in 1993, as a rumba. This was the first of six versions of the song that can be associated to Los Del Rio. Another version, a new flamenco rumba pop fusion theme with fully Spanish lyrics, attained significant success in Spain and Mexico. It also became popular in Puerto Rico because of its use as an unofficial campaign theme song for then-governor Pedro Rosselló, who was seeking reelection under the New Progressive Party of Puerto Rico's ticket. Being the base for many cruise ships, many visitors to the island were constantly exposed to the song during their stay in Puerto Rico. Arguably this explains how the song spread to - and become a smash hit in cities with sizeable Latino communities in the United States, particularly Miami and New York City.

After being remixed by the Bayside Boys and having English lyrics added, it became a worldwide hit in summer 1996. The single spent weeks at number one on the U.S. Billboard Hot 100 singles chart, one of the longest runs atop the Hot 100 chart in history. During its heyday, the song was played frequently at professional athletic games, rallies, conventions, and other places. The Macarena remained popular through 1996, but by the end of 1997, its popularity had diminished greatly. The song also broke records at the time by remaining in the Hot 100 chart for 60 weeks.

The song was also covered by Los del Mar, which was first released in 1995 and then again at the same time as the original in the United Kingdom in the hope of fooling people into buying their version by mistake. It missed the top 40 but the Los del Rio version peaked at number two.

The song was also covered by Doc Watson with an old time country bluegrass group called The Groove Grass Boyz.

As of 1997, the song had sold 11 million copies. While only having a 25% take in royalties from the song, Romero and Ruiz became *immensely wealthy (According to the BBC's News Services, during the year 2003 -a full decade after the song's initial release- Romero and Ruiz made USD $250,000 in royalties during that year alone). Julio Iglesias is quoted as congratulating the duo personally: "My success singing in English from Miami is nothing compared to yours; coming out of Dos Hermanas with little international exposure elsewhere and selling these many records in Spanish takes two huge sets of cojones."*

In VH1's 2002 documentary 100 Greatest One-hit Wonders, Macarena was ranked as #1. Also on a different VH1 documentary, 40 Awesomely Bad No. 1 Songs, Macarena was ranked #1.

-----*wikipedia*

I started as a DJ when the frenzy over the Macarena was dying down. I saw it at done a wedding, years before I ever started playing it. I also saw it performed at an outdoor concert at a local summer festival but I didn't pay too much attention too it. I found it a little confusing and I think in all the time I've been a DJ I have only performed the complex hand gestures correctly, two or three times.

I don't even bother to lead my dancers through the gestures because by now most of them can perform them better than I could. To make up for my lack of Macarena skill, my hands go in all different directions with no rhyme or reason, on purpose of course. I cross my arms, slap myself on the head, make my hands look like a fish and wiggle them around. It looks ridiculous but that's the point. I remain Macarena challenged and I like it that way. Compared to some of the odd behavior and gestures I've seen during the Macarena I look like Fred Astaire.

Hey Macarena!

Unchained melody

"Unchained Melody" is a popular song with music by Alex North and lyrics by Hy Zaret. It is one of the most recorded songs of the 20th century, by some counts having spawned over 500 versions in hundreds of different languages

In 1955, North used the music as a theme for the obscure prison film Unchained. Todd Duncan, the baritone who performed in the

147

original Porgy and Bess, sang the vocals for the film soundtrack. Les Baxter (Capitol Records catalog number 3055), released an instrumental version which reached #2. Al Hibbler followed close behind (Decca Records catalog number 29441, with a vocal version that reached #3 on the Billboard charts). He was followed soon after by Jimmy Young whose version hit #1 on the British charts. Roy Hamilton's version (Epic Records catalog number 9102) reached #6, while June Valli (RCA Victor Records catalog number 20-6078) took it to #29. Rockabilly legend Gene Vincent and His Blue Caps recorded it for their second album in 1956 - Vincent's version is played at mid-tempo and features a tremolo picking guitar part. It is also probably the most unusual cover version, as the chorus was omitted. Harry Belafonte sang it at the 1956 Academy Awards where it finished fifth in the voting for the Academy Award for Best Original Song of 1955. In 1963, an uptempo, doo-wop version hit the regional charts (eastern U.S.) by Vito & the Salutations, eventually becoming part of the soundtrack for Goodfellas in 1990.

The song regained popularity when another version was produced by Phil Spector in 1965, credited to the Righteous Brothers, but performed as a solo by Bobby Hatfield, who later recorded versions credited solely to him. It climbed to #4. "Unchained Melody" reappeared on the Billboard charts in 1990, reaching #19, after The Righteous Brothers' recording was used in the film Ghost. It reached #1 in the UK, becoming the UK's top selling single of 1990; it also later reached #1 in Australia, staying at number-one for 7 weeks through November 1990 and into January 1991.

On June 21, 1977, just six weeks prior to his death, Elvis Presley performed "Unchained Melody" for what would be his last television appearance, "Elvis In Concert." However, the recording that was ultimately released as a single and included on the "Moody Blue" album (the last released while he was alive) was from an earlier appearance at Ann Arbor, Michigan, featuring him on piano, as it was invariably the case when Presley sang the song in concert.

In 1995, the song was performed by Robson Green and Jerome Flynn in the UK drama series Soldier Soldier. This version was subsequently released as a single and quickly reached #1 in the UK, becoming one of the country's all time biggest selling records.

I'm getting a bad reception

The song has become a favorite among auditioners for TV singing contests. It has often been said by Simon Cowell to be his favorite song, leading it to be a favourite among those hoping to impress him in auditions for Pop Idol, American Idol, and The X Factor. It was performed on the original series of Pop Idol by runner-up Gareth Gates, who later released it as a single. It was also sung on Australian Idol by finalist Dan England and 2006's winner Damien Leith, and on American Idol by Clay Aiken during the Season 2 Top 3 finals, after which he advanced to the Top 2 (finals), as well as Kellie Pickler on Season 5 Top 6 Love Songs Week, for which she was eliminated.

In 2004 Rolling Stone placed the song at #365 on their list of The 500 Greatest Songs of All Time.

Cyndi Lauper was nominated for a 2005 Grammy award for "Best Instrumental Composition Accompanying a Vocal" for her interpretation of the song, which appears on the At Last album. In 2006, singer Barry Manilow covered the song on his album Greatest Songs of the Fifties, and it reached #20.

The song has been #1 on lists of love songs featured on Channel Four and Channel Five.

This beautiful tune fills the dance floor every time I play it. It is a dreamy, romantic ballad that is a nice change of pace from the faster portion of the evening. This is one of the first slow songs I play at a wedding reception.

The tune regained popularity in the 80's when it was featured prominently in the film *Ghost*. In a memorable scene, *Unchained Melody* plays in the background as Demi Moore sits working a sculpture on a potters wheel when Patrick Swayze cozies up behind her in a hot, passionate love scene.

The same scene was ruthlessly parodied in the movie *Naked Gun*. This time, Leslie Nielsen and Priscilla Presley recreate the scene frame by frame until of course the potters wheel starts spinning out of control and wet clay flies off the wheel covering everything in sight.

Y. M. C. A.

"Y.M.C.A." is a 1978 song by the Village People which became a

hit in January 1979.

The song reached #2 on the U.S. charts in early 1979 and reached #1 in the UK around the same time, becoming the group's biggest hit ever.

Taking the song at face value, its lyrics extol the virtues of the Young Men's Christian Association. In the gay culture from which the group sprang, the song was understood as celebrating the YMCA's reputation as a popular cruising and hookup spot, particularly for the younger gay men to whom it was addressed (ironically, at the time that the song was a hit, the gay community both increased its visibility and no longer felt the need to use organizations such as the YMCA as a cover for its sexual activities, and the YMCA moved toward being a more family-oriented and less exclusively male organization).

The song has continued to remain popular despite (or later, because of) its status as a disco classic and gay anthem, even among listeners who are otherwise uninvolved in disco or gay culture. A popular dance in which the arms are used to spell out the four letters of the song's title may have much to do with this. It is frequently played during breaks in the action at sporting events, with crowds using the dance as an opportunity to stretch, similar to the later "Macarena".

"Y.M.C.A." is number 7 on VH1's list of The 100 Greatest Dance Songs of the 20th Century.

Producer Henri Belolo recalls that he saw the YMCA sign while walking down the street with composer Jacques Morali, who seemed to know the institution fairly well: "Henri, let me tell you something. This is a place where a lot of people go when they are in town. And they get good friends and they go out." And Henri got the idea: "Why don't we write a song about it?"

The song became a number one hit in many places (notably not in the United States where it lost to Rod Stewart's "Da Ya Think I'm Sexy?"). It has remained popular at parties, events, and functions ever since.

Origin of hand movement & dance:
"YMCA" is also the name of a group dance with cheerleader Y-M-C-A choreography invented to fit the song. One of the phases involves

moving arms to form the letters Y-M-C-A as they are sung in the chorus:

Y - *Arms outstretched and raised*

M - *Made by bending the elbows from the 'Y' pose so the fingertips meet over the chest*

C - *Arms extended to the left*

A - *Hands held together above head*

Dick Clark takes credit for his show American Bandstand being where the YMCA dance was originated. During the January 6, 1979 episode which featured the Village People as the guests throughout the hour, the dance is seen being done by audience members during the performance of YMCA and lead singer Victor Willis is seen practicing the dance himself at the beginning of the standard interview sequence.

At Yankee Stadium, after the fifth inning, the grounds crew traditionally takes a break from grooming the infield to lead the crowd in the dance. Similarly at Sapporo Dome, during Hokkaido Nippon-Ham Fighters baseball games, YMCA is enthusiastically enjoyed by the crowd and ground staff during the fifth inning stretch.

------------wikikpedia

The YMCA is an amazing by product of the disco era. I think it as popular today as it was when it was first blasted out of sound systems at roller rinks and at Studio 54 back in the 1970's. If there is a golden rule book for DJ's, one of the top ten rules would be *'Thou shalt play the YMCA.'*

The *YMCA* is a fun party song that is as cheesy as a plate of hot nachos. The song is a tremendous crowd magnet that draws wayward dancers back to the floor. If there is ever a lull in the action, all it takes is for me to play the first three notes of the *YMCA* and there will be shrieks of delight followed by a mad rush of dancers. It is amazing that this salute to the Young Men's Christian Association (as well as a campy ode to the alternative lifestyle) has such staying power.

There is not a lot for the dancers to do during the verses except bob up and down or step to the left of the right and wait for the chorus. I have seen dancers make a fist with thumbs up and wave their right arm, then their left back and forth across their chest which make them look like they are hitch hiking.

I have also seen variations of the Batusi. This is a play on the Watusi. You make a peace sign on each hand and hold the open fingers over your eyes. This was made famous in the campy 1960's TV version of *Batman.* The Batusi was also performed on screen by John Travolta and Uma Therman in the movie *Pulp Fiction.*

After all these years it is amusing to see dancers in action during this song. I'll never forget good old Melvin from back in the singles group. He liked to dance to this song but was clueless on how to do the hand gestures. When the chorus came, his hands would shoot into the air like he was being robbed at gunpoint at a 7 – 11. His *YMCA* came out something like 'Q', 'X', Ampersand, and something from the Hebrew of Sanskrit languages.

And finally.....

Most of this book was dedicated to wedding receptions and a few class reunions thrown in for good measure. In case you were wondering, or even if you weren't, I have played parties for other occasions, specifically holiday parties.

I save the holiday parties for some pretty special people. In the school district where I live, there are a few classrooms full of special needs kids. The other group consists of special needs adults who live in local adult foster care homes. I drive many or most of those fine folks on my bus during any given week. I drive the adults to their workshop four days a week. I have a special place in my heart for all of those people.

I volunteer my time and play music for their Halloween, Christmas and other parties. Those folks appreciate the music so much. One of 'my guys' loves the music so much he starts dancing before I even have the sound system plugged in. Another loves Elvis music and I make it a point to play something from The King. Yet another loves the Dixie Chicks and Shania Twain and I always make sure I play a few hits from them. He also likes the *Flying Purple People Eater* song so I always put that on for him at Halloween.

It does my heart good to know that I have brought some happiness and joy to their lives. And if I know that I've made somebody happy with my music, I have done my job as a DJ and that makes my time on this Big Blue Marble we live on, worthwhile. And if I have made you laugh or smile while reading this book, then I have done my job as an author as well.

That about wraps it up for this book.

I thank you for reading it. I thank you for your time. And it looks like I have to hit the road and play another party.

I wish you well and until we meet again, I'll see you out on the dance floor.

Matt Engel
A. K. A. The Music and M. E. Disc Jockey Service
P. O. Box 1013
Gaylord, Michigan 49735

www. Mattengel. org

Appendix

The Music and M. E. Disc Jockey – Wedding forms
Disc Jockey Contract

Name _____

Address _____

_____

Thank you for considering THE MUSIC AND ME as the entertainment for your upcoming party. I am honored to play for you. I am dedicated to making the big day as fun, memorable and worry free as possible.

Date of this party

Indicate location of this party

When do I?

Begin playing dance music (estimated time)

Stop playing music (estimated time)

Payment for disc jockey services

A down payment of (X-Amount) is due at the time of booking. Remaining balance of (X-amount) is due no later than (Date of party)

Please make checks payable to:

Yours truly   Somewhere in   Michigan USA

Refund policy

Full refund – Given if for some reason I am forced to cancel

Half refund – Given if YOU cancel up to 30 days before party

No refund – Given if YOU cancel 29 days or less before party

Matthew Engel__Matthew Engel__Your name here_Your name here

154

Please print clearly

How do you want to be introduced when you enter the hall, as well as for your first dance?

I will say 'Ladies and gentlemen, please welcome_____'

(i.e. Mr. And Mrs. Smith or Mr. And Mrs. John Smith or Mr. And Mrs. John and Jane Smith)

Bride and Groom's first dance

Song requested_____Artist_____

Will there be a Bridal Party dance?   Yes_____No_____

If so please print clearly the names of the Bridal Party:

Bridesmaid_____Escorted by Groomsman_____

Bridesmaid_____Escorted by Groomsman_____

Bridesmaid_____Escorted by Groomsman_____

Bridesmaid_____Escorted by Groomsman_____

Bridal Party Dance

Song requested_____Artist_____

Disc Jockey forms - Continued

Please print clearly

Will there be a Father/ Daughter dance?   Yes_____No_____

If so please indicate Father's name:_____

Song requested_____Artist_____

*****

Will there be a Mother/ Son dance?   Yes_____No_____

If so please indicate Mother's name:_____

Song requested_____Artist_____

*****

Will there be a Dollar dance?_____

Will there be a bouquet toss?_____

Will there be a garter toss?_____

Other special events?_____

Disc Jockey forms – Continued

List the songs you like. Use the following lines to tell me what songs you love and would make your party extra special. I will do everything I can to accommodate you.

_____

_____

_____

_____

_____

_____

List the songs you dislike. Everyone has one. The song that makes your flesh crawl. The song that you never want to hear again. Use the following lines to tell me about these as well.

_____

_____

_____

_____

_____

Please list any and all special announcements you would like me to make.

_____

_____

_____

Disc Jockey forms - Continued

Please print clearly

Will there be a Father/ Daughter dance? Yes_____No_____

If so please indicate Father's name:_____

Song requested_____Artist_____

* * * * *

Will there be a Mother/ Son dance?   Yes_____No_____

If so please indicate Mother's name:_____

Song requested_____Artist_____

* * * * *

Will there be a Dollar dance?_____

Will there be a bouquet toss?_____

Will there be a garter toss?_____

Other special events?_____

The music and M. E. – Basic wedding script

Bride and Groom arrive at the hall:
      Matt: Ladies and gentlemen_____

Bride and groom's first dance:
      Matt: And now, to dance their very first dance as husband and wife, please welcome to the dance floor _____

Music Cue: (Example) 'Making memories of us' by Keith Urban

Bridal Party dance:
      Matt: At this time, please welcome to the floor, the ladies of the bridal party and their escorts for the bridal party dance.
      Bridesmaid_____Escorted by_____

Music Cue: (Example) 'Unchained melody' Righteous Brothers

Father/Daughter dance:
      Matt: And now for the Father – Daughter dance, may we please have (Bride) and her father (Father) on the floor for this very special dance.

Music Cue: (Example) 'Daddy's hands' by Holly Dunn

Mother/Son dance:
      Matt: And now for the Mother – Son dance, may we please have (Groom) and his mother (Mother) on the floor for this very special dance.

Music Cue: (Example) 'Wonderful world' by Louis Armstrong

The songs listed above are samples of what I have played at other receptions. I left them in as an example.

Disc Jockey forms – Continued

Cake cutting:
> Matt: And now in honor or (Bride) and (Groom) cutting the wedding cake I have this special tune.

Music cue: 'Sugar sugar' by the Archie's

Bouquet toss:
> Matt: And now it is time for (Bride) to throw the bouquet, we need all the single ladies on the dance floor at this time. So come on ladies get out those catcher's mitts and put on those running shoes, it is time to toss the bouquet. (Bride) when I count to three, you let the bouquet fly. One, two, three! Go!

Garter removal:
> Matt: And now it is time for (Groom) to remove the garter, and in honor of such a serious moment I offer you this serious song.

Music cue: 'The Stripper' by David Rose

Garter toss:
> Matt: And now it is time for (Groom) to throw the garter, we need all the single guys on the floor at this time. So come on guys, don't be shy; it's time to toss the garter. Okay (Groom) when I count to three you let the garter go. One! Two! Three! Go!

Garter guy – bouquet gal dance:
> And now, the young man who caught the garter will place it on the young lady who caught the bouquet and they'll have their own dance.

Music cue: 'Crazy' by Patsy Cline

Disc Jockey forms – Continued

What follows is a sample list of the music that I will be playing and have played at several weddings and parties. This is not of course written in stone and is quite flexible. The music is played during the faster music / portion of the evening. It comes after the following typical lineup for a wedding reception.

I play what I call a good three / three mix. Three fast songs, three slow, the mix is pop / rock / country and hip-hop.

I – Dinner music

Slower, softer music played in the background during cocktails and conversation.

II – Dinner

III – Specialty dances

Bride and groom's first dance

Bridal party dance

Father / Daughter dance

Mother / Son dance

IV – Dancing

Disc Jockey forms – Continued

Typical dance line up

Fast -	Old time rock and roll	Bob Seger
	Play something country	Brooks n Dunn
	Everybody dance now	C + C Music factory
Slow –	Unchained melody	Righteous brothers
	Who's gonna hold you tonight?	Trace Adkins
	I swear	All 4 One
Fast –	Dancing Queen	ABBA
	I wanna talk about me	Toby Keith
	Cha Cha Slide	Mr. C
Slow –	Crazy	Patsy Cline
	How deep is your love	Bee Gees
	Breathe	Faith Hill
Fast –	You shook me all night long	ACDC
	Sweet home Alabama	Lynyrd Skynyrd
	Let's get married	Jagged Edge
Slow –	After all	Cher/Peter Cetera
	Amazed	Lonestar
	Wonderful tonight	Eric Clapton
Fast –	YMCA	Village People
	Chicken Dance	Emeralds
	Locomotion	Little Eva
Slow –	Could I have this dance?	Anne Murray
	Layla	Eric Clapton
	Remember when	Alan Jackson
Fast –	Don't leave me this way	Thelma Houston
	You're my better half	Keith Urban
	My humps	Black eyed peas

Slow - Easy like Sunday morning	**Commodores**
Must be doing something right	**Billy Currington**
Three times a lady	**Commodores**
Fast – Hit me with your best shot	**Pat Benetar**
Billy got his beer goggles on	**Neal McCoy**
Miss New Booty	**Bubba Sparxx**
Slow – To make you feel my love	**Garth Brooks**
Stand by me	**The Drifters**
Unanswered prayers	**Garth Brooks**
Fast – Walk like an Egyptian	**The Bangles**
Red dirt road	**Brooks n Dunn**
Pon de replay	**Rihanna**
Slow – Out of my head	**Fastball**
Your man	**Josh Turner**
I'll be	**KC & Jo Jo**
Fast – Love shack	**B 52's**
Goodbye Earl	**Dixie Chicks**
Hips don't lie	**Shakira**
Slow – Memories of us	**Keith Urban**
Kiss from a rose	**Seal**
What I need to do	**Kenny Chesney**
Fast – My Sharona	**The Knack**
Honky Tonk Badonkadonk	**Trace Adkins**
Yeah	**Usher**
Slow - Waterfalls	**TLC**
When I said 'I do'	**Clint Black**
At last	**Etta James**
Fast – Takin' care of business	**BTO**
Tainted love	**Soft cell**
Nice and slow	**Usher**

Slow – She's my kind of rain	Tim McGraw
New York state of mind	Billy Joel
Then they do	Trace Adkins
Fast – Bad bad Leroy Brown	Jim Croce
Bad boys	Glora Estevan
Hot blooded	Foreigner
Slow - Lights	Journey
Open arms	Journey
My wish	Rascal Flatts
Fast – Centerfold	J. Geils Band
Summer nights	Grease Cast
You're the one that I want	Grease Cast
Slow – Heaven	Brian Adams
The Rose	Bette Midler
Drift away	Doby Gray
Fast – Tequila	The Champs
Rock this town	Stray Cats
Macarena	Los Del Mar
Slow – What a wonderful world	Louis Armstrong
Home	Michael Buble
At this moment	Billy Vera
Fast – Respect	Aretha Franklin
Shout	Isley Brothers
Mickey	Toni Basil
Slow – Have I told you lately?	Van Morrison
You are so beautiful	Joe Cocker
Live to tell	Madonna
Fast – I love rock and roll	Joan Jett
Hurts so good	John Mellencamp
Jack and Dianne	John Mellencamp

Slow – All my life   **KC & Jo Jo**
  One more night   **Phil Collins**
  Dust in the wind   **Kansas**

Fast – Brown eyed girl   **Van Morrison**
  My life   **Billy Joel**
  Still rock and roll to me   **Billy Joel**

Slow – Lean on me   **Bill Withers**
  Behind closed doors   **Charlie Rich**
  Come in from the rain   **Captain and Tennille**

Fast – She drives me crazy   **Fine young cannibals**
  Crazy little thing called love   **Cheap trick**
  You spin me round   **Dead or alive**

Last song – Last Dance   **Donna Summer**
Encore – Goodnight sweetheart   **The Spaniels**

Read all about it

Amazon.com

Kidzworld.com

Hudson Valley Weddings. Com

The American Wedding. Com

The Wedding Channel Com

Wikipedia. Org